D1245947

Doc and the Judge

Sex, Drugs, Rock 'N' Roll
& A One-Eyed Scratch Golfer

By Gary M. Granger

Doc and the Judge: Sex, Drugs, Rock 'N' Roll & A One-Eyed Scratch Golfer
Copyright© 2008 by Reality Press and Gary M. Granger. All rights reserved.

No part of this book may be reproduced or transmitted in any form or by any means, graphic, electronic, or mechanical, including photocopying, recording, taping or by any information storage or retrieval system, without permission in writing from the publisher at: info@reality-entertainment.com.

Reality Press
An imprint of Reality Entertainment, Inc.

For information contact:

REALITY ENTERTAINMENT
P.O. Box 91
Foresthill, CA 95631

Ph: 530-367-5389
Fx: 530-367-3024

www.reality-entertainment.com

ISBN: 978-1-934588-42-0
Printed in the United States of America.

Contents

Doc and the Judge

Dedication

This book is dedicated to Jackie Milner a pioneer in modern FM Radio. She forged a way for others who followed. Her legendary, inspirational successes paved the way for a new generation of women for whom she revealed broadcasting as a real career opportunity in the industry we love.

I posthumously thank and give thanks to the Judge for the amazing ride he took me on. His vision and recipe for life were shocking, moving, humbling and magical all at once; it also goes a long way to explaining his legendary lust for life. Those years with the Judge helped to forge my soul and spirit into what I consider to be the essence of the man I am today: a very lucky, contented and good gentleman with killer memories.

I extend a heartfelt thank you to my beautiful daughter Kristina whose enduring love, goodness and support have filled both my heart and my life with ecstatic meaning. Thanks to my beautiful wife Elena who's tenacious, purposeful spirit and perseverance helped a first time writer endure the withering toil that is the road to publication. I am a truly blessed man. I'd like to thank Larry England and Rod Crews for their friendship, support and golfing dudeness.

Finally I'd like to praise and give thanks in equal portion for my mother Flo and my father Buck under who's humility, wisdom and guidance their children were sent out into the world with the simple message urging they seek to, "improve it for others and the next generation," at best and to "do no harm" at worst. Their deepest abiding instinct for us was to be a positive influence in the world we inhabit. In closing I'd honor my darling little sister Josephine who did not live long enough to leave the entire world breathless with her goodness as she did us on a daily basis. My brothers Kenneth and Mark stand beside me on the perfection that she was, a true Angel on Earth for a few dazzling years.

Doc and the Judge

Introduction - The View

"I can see for miles and miles and….."

I'm writing this story perched about 2000 feet high in a gloriously tranquil home facing "west south west" in the Sierras, perfectly tucked away atop a mountain in a delightful Californian 49'ers gold town called Sonora. I pause and contemplate my next thought as I shell pistachios and sip Laughing Magpie vintage 2004, a robust Australian Shiraz. When I write in the afternoon I plan a break to allow me to be on the deck and in the spa to enjoy every sumptuously vivid gathering sunset. I've never tired of the glory of the sun drifting languidly toward the horizon through the course of the day then in one magnificent heartbeat vanishing in a breathtaking violet glow.

With the Judge's ever present spirit about me as I move through my day, now is the time to seek out my spot marking the nexus between two wooden posts on the deck. It's here that I settle to observe the sun, and mark its relative height off the horizon. Though I confess I'm but a novice in such matters, I've boldly calculated the sun's comparative drop in relation to time and distance from the horizon. Finally, I measure this quotient against the notches carved onto the deck's posts whereupon I'm lead confidently to a powerful conviction in the sun doing exactly what it should at precisely the right time every day. The glory of God surrounds us yet we so seldom have the time, inclination or indeed opportunity to stop and survey, much less fully take in this awe inspiring majesty. From my rather modest vantage point, planet earth is doing just fine.

I hope for a time in the near future when our collective consciousness compels us, or better yet shames us, into forging a covenant with our Earth to care for her as she nurtures us; she too is a living organism. Put quite simply, we all perish if she herself was to face peril.

The Judge enjoys the view; I hear the echo in the canyons of my mind of his bellowing and jubilant shouts of "rock 'n' roll." It's as if he wants to drown out thoughts in me he finds too serious and somber, in short, thoughts not of the dude language we shared. I clear my head and continue down the path of today's thoughts while assuring the Judge I haven't lost the spirit and beg his continued indulgence on this journey.

The closest city lights visible are far enough away to serve as bearings on the horizon in the flawless evening sky. They're barely noticed though they do in their own way make a bold statement like a lightly jeweled necklace an elegant woman of means favors to softly adorn her lustrous skin. Everything in between is pleasing. The happily situated smattering of cottages and farms mercifully all remain closer to the distant city lights than to me and my hilltop reverie.

I can see for miles and miles from the Sonora deck!

This, my friend is the view. I found it a few years ago while on a national tour promoting breast cancer awareness for young women with my wife Mari. She was diagnosed with terminal breast cancer at age 29. Wherever we travelled I remember noting that even a cursory glance of mine across any one of those crowded waiting rooms and I'd feel we surely must be amidst expectant mothers. There were so many young, vibrant, beautiful women who only upon closer scrutiny betrayed their crushing anguish. The stunned look of first diagnosis burned ever present in their eyes. Some wore wigs while bald statements preferred by others, nonetheless all these young women in various stages of treatment for this horribly sneaky disease strove to live normal, fulfilling lives with whatever time remained for each of them.

Mari died at the age of 35 in this village surrounded by friends and family who held her hand to the end just as she'd held the hands of hundreds around the country offering each solace in their final hour. I now live in Sonora permanently; it's been my place of healing and contemplation.

As we grow older we each gain experience and learn from experiences shared by others. It's clear we take our memories with us and keep them close wherever we choose to be. How did we get here? How do we convince the person in the mirror that he should be wearing this face? What vexing questions these are. The Judge says it doesn't look much like me and truthfully even to me it doesn't seem much like me so who could it be?

I believe what we see in the mirror is us. Put simply this is who we are now, better still it manifests who and what we've become. Some feel it's far too late for radical change and perhaps that's so, however it's never too late to pull back the layers, dispense with silly deceptions and begin to be inquisitive about ourselves.

The why's and the how's become polemic. The why nevertheless is easy to answer as it brings us into a broad discussion with our truest self, the how actually seems more complex until we accept why and how are interrelated as they must be.

Take a moment to prominently identify the most important goal in your life right now. Then go slowly back identifying the markers in life that guided your way, you know them; they always stand alone as defining moments. As you identify and seek to understand them then chronologically plot these moments it brings you full circle back to this moment. Your place now is a destination reached as a direct result of every development reached, in every moment lived and through every decision taken. Therefore, what's important to you today was perennially thus.

Memories of the past selected and pulled to the surface play significant roles as they seek to flesh out an understanding of the voyage toward today. In short they've molded us into who we were meant to be, answering why we find ourselves as we do here and now. This process culminates in a focus on, understanding of, and finally an acceptance of who we were before the cata-strophic but no less defining events mapped our course toward our destina-tion. Thus the continuum is perpetuated in us until the next big fork in the road offers us up new directions and possibilities.

On this point I believe every shake up, every welcome and unwelcome dis-ruption in our lives is in and of itself life changing. Be it positive or nega-tive it remains a critical agent of change and lays in wait, positively charged for exponential growth and development in our lives. Ultimately no matter that the foundation of our world may bend, falter, or break down under the burden of change, our lives at that moment have inexorably changed and now propels us into new, exciting directions if only we'll allow this newness to lead us onward. The only bad decision I feel sure is to deny change, thereby deny-ing oneself the possibility to fully explore and adjust robustly to these shifting new landscapes of flux. Change is full of prescience and promise however change denied is fear merely reacting in the guise of action.

Change is unstoppable, to that end to fail to change abreast of change is not an appropriate action nor is it an action of stoicism. In short it's neither a more reasoned nor more rational response. In fact, every day you fail to embrace change is an act of cowardice and betrayal of your potential power to pre-vail over perceived fears. "Break on thru to the other side," was a watershed anthem for change in mesmerizing style sung by Jim Morrison in his 1960's cult hit.

When we identify all those qualities we know we possess and bundle them up and sort them out, only then can we make sense of this data and only after that can we accept we're all fundamentally righteous in our moment on earth. We're riddled with the same faults and frailties humans have always struggled with. We recognize shortcomings but they are fortifying tools to be used as we acknowledge powerful strength flourishes from identified weaknesses if only we'll accept and permit change to permeate our lives from them. Thus, as we begin to understand we can begin to embrace and eventually accept ourselves, only then does the raging battle within begin to subside.

As we seek to know peace with self we must also stand back and honestly as-sess our personal data. We need to look back at the highs as well as the lows, each must be equally weighted against the goals we'd set for ourselves at that time. I think most of us believe we can look back with pride at our accomplishments. We've attempted to right wrongs, raise families and work hard. We feel that we've contributed in some small way to community, country and mankind.

I seek peace. I stare in the mirror as I shave and try to find a little something in my face every day that signals peace may be just around the corner. I yearn for peace. I seek peace with family and friends. I enjoy peace with my animals, my environment, and yes even my God who is now my most constant companion guiding my way, sharing my load and moving me toward the radiant light of peace.

My approach has been to search the barren gaps between defining moments where I seek to search out memories that may have fallen down chasms in between. I don't rely on the recollections of others, instead I choose to go inside seeking to find things that connect to other puzzle parts, then as in a jigsaw I fit them all into their own unique place in my own "work in progress" life.

I discovered a beautiful memory of my mother as a young bride and with a young family of her own sneaking food out every afternoon to leave by the side of the wide alley that separated the backs of houses in my hometown. This alley was visited daily by young black women with their children as they busily sorted through the refuse for food. On their heads they balanced tightly wrapped sheets containing their findings which mostly consisted of food scraps and clothes that could be recycled for their children. Mother would fry extra chicken, hamburgers and so on which she'd carefully wrap in paper and leave in the alley for these mothers and their children.

I also remember my mother's solemn prayers every evening as she whispered passionately to God "My children will never go to bed hungry, they have a wonderful daddy who makes good money but Lord, I know many children do." She'd finish up every night's prayer vigil with this blessing "Dear God, we have enough to get by and I thank you, I thank you for giving us our daily bread and for giving me this family."

My mother was goodness personified. Her goodness was given quietly, discreetly, thoughtfully. It's been a great joy for me to discover during this process her fingerprint evidenced throughout my life; I'm very proud of it and it has served me extremely well. Indeed mother's own sense of generosity and fairness has been the very foundation stone upon which every transaction I entered into during my adult life has been predicated.

It's as if throughout the project of this book she's been sitting by my side reading my mind prompting me and helping me fill in the blanks. She knew all my secrets including the ones that kept her awake at night. Only after she'd been able to reach me by phone (no matter the time of day or night) to confirm that I'd arrived home safely was she able herself to relax and go to sleep. I suspect mothers have done thus down through the ages.

Her daily prayers came to include the safe keeping of her son Doc and his friend the Judge. This story is a meditation on the times and on their lives as they rode the 70's wildly, without fear or favor. They were great friends forever.

When "tomorrow" arrived as it must for us all, it was a shock akin to a rude interruption by an uninvited party guest; we each dealt with it in our own way. The Judge just wanted to shut the door on this boorish guest. I recognized early on he was neither ready for nor interested in the promise of a million tomorrows. For me tomorrow snuck in while I was too busy to notice and now I sit here on my deck with another glorious sunset ablaze and ponder. No doubt I've mellowed. I concede. I sit here on the deck again on this brilliant evening as I reflect back on those extraordinary days of bell bottom jeans, gravity defying afros, those wicked sky high times. Hoochie Coo!

It was the early 70's. The flowery dogma of the sixties was finally dimming. Woodstock became a more distant memory every day though a kernel of its heady spirit lived on and will in perpetuity as it was indeed a seminal moment in the culture of this nation. The Woodstock generation was the most powerful unified voice of change modern America has experienced. It stopped a war as it gave voice to a generation that agitated for the emancipation of women and minorities. What happened?

Perhaps you'll find some semblance of your own life here. Close your eyes and relax... there. Now open your eyes and relax, now read on… it's important we remain steadfast, focused. This ride goes back to a time of great tumult, great joy, incredible and memorable music, deep faith and conviction, along with a smattering of breathtaking recklessness. You're going back to a time where youthful exuberance, skin tight leather pants and unabashed excess were the currency of the day.

The Doc

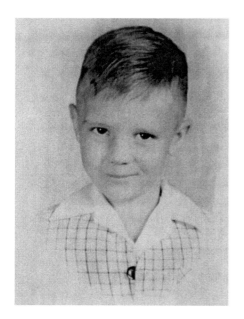

Doc as a first grader in Georgia. The Judge always called Doc "Country Dude."

My life began very humbly. I was born at home in a farmhouse in Georgia; I suspect this is where my enduring love for horses, cows, dogs, cats, chickens, birds and above all the land took hold. The birds then and now know where to come for hearty chow. I delighted in my private little bird sanctuary then as a child in Georgia and I again have the privilege of abundant birdlife living in harmony about me here in California too. My life in Sonora is magical.

I grew up like most, a product of my environment. I was a smart, athletic, freckled-faced, God-fearing boy who early on developed a keen entrepreneurial streak including selling old buttons to old women in the neighborhood, another big revenue raiser was holding bicycle races on a track I'd built in an open field then cheekily charging admission to both participants and spectators for events organized and held there. There were a myriad of other such activities that an entrepreneurial young mind could dream up.

As a fifth grader, the rebellious side of me organized five of my buddies to join me in a runaway to Florida. I convinced them that children in Florida were treated as adults. On our "breakaway" day though the practical side of me watched out of the classroom window as those friends took off on their trek resting hastily gathered belongings and snacks in a pillowcase tied onto the ends of sticks teetering casually over their shoulder.

These young fugitives were quickly picked up by the Sheriff before they made it too far and returned to school in time for lunch. I told them they'd passed the test which was to challenge their courage and I let them know how proud I was of them.

That weekend, as if to declare our coming of age we huddled in a tent behind my house looking at photos by flashlight of naked Asian women that a brother of one of the boys had recently brought back from a military tour of duty. I was the only one to have an erection. They voted unanimously to elect me leader then and there; they echoed in unison that my undeniable and verifiable credentials were proven that evening.

First a born leader as my mother loved to say, then a decisive, verifiable leader that evening. Many left the tent painfully raw due to persevering in the 'can do spirit' that we Americans are famous for. However, on this occasion their energetic attempts lead to an aching, throbbing stinging they all complained of. They all eventually walked home sheepishly in deep shame and very gingerly with pain, each step taken being designed to control the excruciating hot ache.

Every leader needs protection; this new leader's personal protection came from the first of two one-eyed friends in my life to leave an indelible mark, an 11-year-old fighter nicknamed "Cooter," who took on bullies fearlessly, even those who were many years his senior. He'd lost his eye as a child when a cherry bomb firecracker thrown at him by his older brother exploded in his face. On occasion he'd pick fights merely to demonstrate that the leader would always be safe on his watch.

When a fight broke out Cooter would pop his glass eye out of his left eye socket and then he'd toss it to me to hold for a few seconds while he quickly and decisively finished off opponents. Once he tossed me the eye from quite a distance whereupon a sudden wind gust caught it causing it to sail some twenty or thirty feet off target ultimately finding a resting place in some tall weeds which happened to include waist high patches of rabbit tobacco.

Blossoming rabbit tobacco signals the change of seasons from summer to fall and also back-to-school time in the south. The two of us crawled for a long time on all fours in our new back-to-school jeans searching for the glass eye by flashlight. When we finally found it, Cooter cleaned the glass eye with a lick of his tongue then pressed it back into his eye socket.

We relaxed after our scare by sitting back and stuffing rabbit tobacco, which many in the south called "loco weed" or "wacky baca," into a corn cob pipe that Cooter always carried in his back pocket. One toke of the wild weed leaves a lasting memory of its unusual fragrance, a nasty throat burning bite, not to mention a temporary wacky or loco high.

My dad, God rest his soul, once took Cooter and me for a spin in his brand new Ford Victoria. An elderly lady swerved from her side of the road and hit us head on. The impact threw us both over the front seat and Cooter hit his head on the dashboard knocking out his glass eye and also cutting his face. He had blood trickling steadily down his cheeks. The sight and taste of the blood frightened him, he was ashen faced with fear then began shouting loudly and uncontrollably, "Oh, no... I'm dead, I'm dead, I'm dead!"

Dad suggested we get out of the car if we were able, so he could better assess our condition. Once outside the car and with feet now firmly planted back on terra firma Cooter delighted in his apparent unscathed condition. He began chanting uncontrollably, "I'm alive, I'm alive, I'm alive," reminiscent of Dr. Frankenstein about his newly fashioned mythic monster man creation.

By now we also found Cooter's missing glass eye and his spirits were positively jubilant. This tough guy had transformed into a "malt shop double shake" within minutes on that two-lane country road. Long ago I heard that Cooter had broken loose from the Georgia chain-gang. Hope he made it!

By the time I was 12, I was also having continuous problems with my tonsils, so near my twelfth birthday I'm taken to hospital for a tonsillectomy. The surgery is successful and I'm back in bed and on my very groggy road to recovery.

My father enters the room only to find a larger than my slight frame bulk under my blanket. He's perplexed and concerned. I believe he pulled back the covers with the intention of adjusting my bedding.

What he found however was in equal part a feisty and lusty young nurse whose now wild, frightened eyes are peering back at him in abject terror. His mind is racing to make sense of the scene before him. I was groggy and smiling broadly from ear to proverbial ear, she was scared, scandalous and titillating!

My father let us both know in his no nonsense style that we were both in big trouble. He asked her to leave the room. He kept his cool while giving me a stern look of foreboding. Within minutes however his demeanor cracked revealing a wide appreciative grin. Then we chuckled over the incident. He was proud of his son scoring at such a tender age. In another time he'd have high-fived me. Imagine that young nurse is now in her seventies and probably still working her little heart out to bring her unique brand of joy to ailing souls somewhere, unless of course she's in jail for her highly unorthodox medical care.

I stayed with my grandmother a lot while growing up. She'd care for me when mother and daddy were away with my sister at hospitals in Atlanta. She had the music and the Lord himself in her and she'd pound away gospel songs on the piano late into the night as long as I could stay awake and clap.

On drives with her I'd stuff myself into the area of the back window behind the seat of her car where I could look out the window at the stars while listening to The Grand Ole Opry on WSM out of Nashville. She and I shared this station and we always referred to it as "our" station.

Once I asked her to play a couple of songs for me on the piano. One was *Running Bear* and the other was *Sixteen Tons*. I played the songs for her on a little record player I'd been given so she'd know the tunes I wanted her to play. However she understood the words to *Running Bear* to be "Running Bear loves little white girl" instead of white dove, which ruffled her deep southern feathers. To add insult to injury when I played *Sixteen Tons*, things deteriorated immediately when she heard the line, "You owe your soul to the company store."

She angrily smashed both records and snapped vehemently, "Never listen to music singing of black boys or Indians loving white girls." She railed on with righteous indignation, "More importantly young man, your soul is owed to Jesus – the Good Lord and no one else, certainly not to any company store and don't you forget that, never let anyone tell you otherwise."

She was resting in the bedroom as I was leaving to host my first emcee job.

She wished me the best and crossed her fingers for my good luck. When I returned around midnight and went into her room to say goodnight she was sound asleep with her fingers still crossed. I've always kept a picture of her close by. She's been my moral compass.

I learned charity first hand when it came time for my older sister, Josephine, to have a heart operation to repair a congenital hole in the heart. She was to be the first person in Atlanta at age 13 to have this operation and it was seen as the only way to give her a normal life. Mother wanted so much for her daughter to be able to run and play with her friends.

There was no health insurance to speak of for textile workers in Georgia in the 50's, my sister's surgeons nonetheless agreed to do the heart surgery for a small fee due to the urgent circumstances. Mother and daddy had no money, nor would they ask anyone for help. Money was saved and whatever we came up short would be paid in time to the doctors.

I remember coming home from school in the car with mother and my sister and the ritual of mother walking up to the mailbox then coming back with envelopes full of cash. There were never names attached to the gifts. Families knew of my sister's upcoming operation and in utter goodness people helped neighbors in need. We never knew who the money came from but we always knew we were surrounded by good and kind people; this was just further evidence as if any was needed of true kindness.

I remember hearing mother crying every night as the date of the surgery approached. I'd hear her prayers knowing she'd prostrate herself before God begging that He intervene in the life of her little girl. On the day before the surgery and on the way to the hospital mother and daddy brought my sister by the school to say goodbye. Daddy gave me five dollars and told me that my grandmother would pick me up after school to care for my brother and me until they returned home with our sister. My grandfather had just bought me a genuine wool baseball suit just like my heroes the Atlanta Crackers wore. I couldn't wait for Josephine to see me in it!

Meanwhile at the hospital mother walks briskly alongside the gurney down corridors continuing to hold my sister's hand, she's told they'd have to ask her to wait in the room assuring her that her little girl would be delivered back there in a few hours. Soon afterwards however they're back, mother panics, instinctively knowing the doctors couldn't be finished and that they'd returned too soon. It had only been two hours since her daughter was taken for surgery. She knew something was terribly wrong, she starting begging the doctors to bring her girl back to the room.

The doctors tell mother that when they opened Josephine's little chest, they discovered she was not physically ready yet for the operation. They told mother they realized she needed to grow some more and that she'd probably be ready for the operation in a couple of years. They then assured mother that my sister would be coming back to her room very soon.

Mother pleaded with them to simply bring her back, she knew things would be fine. The doctors returned again a half hour later to say that little Josephine had died on the operating table. An accident had occurred during the suturing process where an artery had been perforated which they were unable to control and my sister had literally bled to death. Daddy found one of the young surgeons in his office with head in hands crying uncontrollably.

When I visit the family cemetery plot where my sister, mother, father, a child of mine who died at birth, and my wife are buried, I have vivid flashbacks of mother being helped out of a car at Josephine's funeral. She was bent at the waist and broken by her despair, her cries and grasping for breath scared me then and left me feeling the pity she'd felt on that day when I was still too young to understand her raw anguish and driving heart sickness. A flickering reminiscence and I'm back at that mournful day, I can feel the palpable heat on that day I'm transported back to from time to time. I can hear the insects buzzing, and I can smell the ripe fragrance of dry summer grasses. Mostly I can hear my mother's unbridled grief on that hot summer afternoon in August of 1956.

Life was never the same. My sister's room was never touched. Clothes hung in closets as they were left the day of her surgery; the cedar box, all the dolls and personal belongings were lovingly protected and kept up by mother for the rest of her life. Josephine's two pet parakeets died on the same day she did. I buried them near the garden where we used to sit on the ground and do our homework together. Mother lost weight slipping from about 130 pounds to 75 halving her already slight and now frail body. She felt terrible responsibility for her daughter's death because it was her decision to proceed with surgery. She lost her will to live.

Christmas disappeared in our home for many years. Mother couldn't bear to celebrate anything nor decorate trees or do any of the things we'd done as a family for Christmas. Not anymore, not without her little girl. Years later she wept, apologizing to me for taking Christmas away from us. She insightfully waited to apologize until she knew I'd understand.

By now we'd moved to Atlanta. One of my new buddies is a few years older and is offered the family car on this infamous night of Christmas Eve, 1962. He's Jewish, therefore not celebrating Christmas either. At my home we still do nothing for the holidays in deference to Josephine's memory and my mother's inability to celebrate due to the loss of her little girl. The two of us decided to drive to the city and hang out. For some reason tonight was the night to visit "our" favorite radio station, WQXI, "Quixie in Dixie."

After banging at the door of the studios for what seemed to be an eternity the door finally creaked opened slightly revealing a pallid, sallow looking figure who welcomed us in a very deep ominous voice crystallizing a flash back in my mind of images of Vincent Price. He seemed very surprised to see us and genuinely wondered why a couple of kids would be banging on his door on Christmas Eve?

We told him we wanted to meet the person on the radio. He asked us to wait. After a few minutes the door opened again. A portly, jolly and effervescent type of fellow came to the door. After a quick introduction he gave us the once over then invited us in. It was our favorite disc-jockey Hot Rod Roddy! He took us into the studio where we watched him do his show until midnight. He took us out for a burger afterward and that night a new life began for me.

Just as priests describe having a calling, just as athletes dream of making it to the big leagues, and just as every politician aspires to the Presidency, at that moment I knew I'd be a DJ! Not a doctor, an attorney, a baseball player, not a fireman, not fighter pilot, not a race car driver, a disc-jockey.

I gave up everything, school, sports, hanging out with friends and chose instead to take a bus across town every night to the radio station to watch and learn. I was just 14. In April 1963, I landed on the payroll as the switchboard operator for Roddy's show. I voraciously read everything about radio while simultaneously and particularly desperately practiced my speech modulation with the hopes of neutralizing my southern accent.

I followed Roddy to concerts, to record hops, bar mitzvah's, and other DJ events. He told me once over dinner that he was gay. I told him that I wasn't and the subject was buried forever except on occasion when he'd want to boast about exploits, and I generously obliged.

Once while on the road Roddy picked up a hitchhiker who was pushed into the back of the car by his companion from behind him. After they were both in they pulled a gun forcing Roddy to drive to a wooded area where they were going to rob and possibly kill him … until he told them who he was. He was the famous Hot Rod Roddy, the nighttime DJ. They kicked him in the stomach, beat him up, then kicked him out of his car and left him naked in the woods. They stole his car, a 1950 black Pontiac that didn't have a back seat. A few days later they returned the car to the parking lot of the radio station. Roddy sold me the car for a dollar. Understandably, he never wanted to see it again, so his reject became my first set of wheels. Not long after this I landed my own show on Sunday mornings and suffice it to say that many girls in school wanted a ride in my "hot rod."

It was an interesting time for a young, small town, southern boy to be in Atlanta. It was the beginning of race riots, drugs, activism and all this set in the context of an economic boom for the city. As a cub reporter, I'd leave a meeting with Governor Lester Maddox and drive to a meeting with Dr. Martin Luther King. I covered a Maddox rally in Harlem, Georgia one night where I witnessed people getting riled up after a Maddox speech then they were sold ax handles. I followed two guys out of the venue and watched them beat up the first black person they came across, a shocking, cruel, pack mentality which dehumanized the individual, hurting and possibly killing innocent people.

The first direct racial scare I experienced was one night when I missed the last bus across town after work and I was forced to walk through the streets of downtown Atlanta to the freeway near the Capitol where I knew I could hitch a ride. I watched two young black men mercilessly beat up a white kid. I hid in the entranceway of a National Shirt Shop until it was safe to move on. I was now 15.

I remember having a few private moments with Dr. King at the Atlanta premier of the movie Dr. Zhivago. One of my jobs at the station was to produce the Sunday morning public affairs show; Dr. King was a regular guest there so he knew me well. When I got to the lobby to buy popcorn Dr. King incredibly was standing there all alone. I admired him deeply as a leader and a visionary. I'd memorized many of his speeches by the time I was 17. We talked for a few minutes then I asked if I might bring my date up to meet him. Although he said yes, by the time the two of us returned to the lobby he was surrounded by people. He held his hand to his ear as if holding a phone, which meant that I should call him.

I was attending radio school for my 1st Class Radio License the day Dr. King was assassinated. When the announcement of his death came over the intercom, there was a standing ovation from all the students except one. I left the room and never returned.

Roddy went on to an illustrious career that included acting, announcer for the popular TV series Soap, and for the game show The Price Is Right....come on down! Mostly, however, he remained an all out advocate for the extreme. He was a friend and great mentor. He graciously drove hours to attend my grandmother's funeral. He died of colon and breast cancer in 2003.

I came back to Atlanta radio after the Marines then moved to follow my dreams with an offer for nights on a radio station in Detroit. If not for that move I would likely have never met the Judge. I left Atlanta loaded with what I thought would be enough memories to last a lifetime. I assured myself I'd packed in a lot of living the past five years. I'd experienced my first taste of "stagger juice" when the great Charlie Rich (I had no idea at the time who he was and certainly after several drinks it wouldn't have mattered if it had been Abe Lincoln himself) passed a flask to me over his shoulder asking that I pass it on to Del Shannon (him I knew from his song *Hats Off To Larry*) who was seated behind me on a bus loaded with the top entertainers of the day en route to a huge outdoor concert at Ponce de Leon ballpark produced by the radio station. Del said, "Go ahead kid, take a hit." And I'd already experienced my first threesome having found myself between the sheets with a groupie and her beautiful recently divorced rich mother in their mansion in a swank area of Atlanta called Buckhead. I was voted the most popular disc jockey in Atlanta by a teen magazine called The Beat, had made what I considered at the time to be zillions of dollars promoting and hosting shows around Atlanta, although not every show was a hit. I remember once having a "split the door" arrangement with Ronnie Millsap when the total take was $40. The show went on as planned and afterwards I offered Ronnie the full $40. He said, "No, buy the band some beer." And I'd experienced the bar scene finding myself in bars with the likes of Otis Redding, Joe South, Wayne Cochran, and other big names of the day. Once a fight broke out at the Whisk A Go Go, (yes "Whisk" because Atlanta ordinances didn't allow the word Whiskey to be used as part of the name of a drinking establishment) when Otis leaned over to kiss a white barmaid on the cheek. Bouncers quickly tossed out some patrons who didn't approve of the affection shown by a black man to a white girl. I had the privilege of being on stage with the Beatles at their appearance at the Atlanta Baseball Stadium, and I was certainly the first in my family to experience the "evil weed." And I always finished my night with a stop at Pig Alley when the Braves were in town. My daddy didn't want to hear my stories of me seeing Joe Torre falling off his bar stool; "It should never be talked about," he said. Now what more could a twenty-year-old ask for? It sure was fun, and little did I know that the fun had just begun.

Whisk A Go Go ad
"from the day."

A few years later in Ft. Lauderdale, the label "Doc" was given to me by a record company rep who found my approach to the radio and music business to be unorthodox in that I was "methodical." "Clinical" was another description often used about my style but by the same token this kind of comprehensive and exacting approach to business was not customary during those formative years of progressive rock on FM.

Meet the Judge

Even before I ever met the Judge there seemed to be an exquisite pre-destiny to it all. The Judge's father had a business partner who was a distinguished, prominent national sportscaster. These men shared many and varied interests including sports, broadcasting, drinking, women, and above all they were both gifted storytellers. For his part, the Sportscaster did 75 play by play games every year including college football, basketball, NFL and the PGA.

The Judge was born a dude!

The Judge's father had been a very popular jazz disc jockey in Philadelphia; his audacious style was matched only by his business acumen though his first love remained sports broadcasting. He was a natural born salesman, a lifelong broadcaster, and I called him the Jazzman. He was negotiator, enforcer, mythmaker, seducer and bankroller all rolled into one. He went out on his own and bought radio stations in Michigan and Iowa, which he sold to team up with the Sportscaster.

The Sportscaster and Jazzman bought radio stations in Florida. The properties were owned by a retired military Colonel who was extremely proud of the service he'd provided the beachside community since settling there. Upon announcing his retirement the Colonel set out to choose his successor. This act while eccentric spoke eloquently of his dedication to the community and surprised no-one who knew of his affection for his town.

Ultimately, even as the Colonel lay quite literally on his death bed, he maintained his commitment to finding the right successor for his stations and by now the Jazzman had become his favorite. Over many late nights they shared musings on the perils of business, commitment to community, religion, life and even death. The Colonel sold Jazzman his beloved radio stations in good conscience.

The Jazzman invested his own money; the Sportscaster was underwritten by the owner of a pro football team. As it was told to me, the Sportscaster's money flowed on a handshake which later became a matter of great chagrin for both men when it transpired that absolutely no formal contract existed. As luck would have it, the Sportscaster suddenly and unexpectedly took ill precipitously passing away whereupon his financial backer immediately called in the loan in question. Well, all hell broke loose since clearly repayment of a loan of this size was impossible in the time demanded. The radio stations were in fact sold, but not before many tumultuous years passed.

The Sportscaster sent me to Florida to work with Jazzman; this came shortly after an incident in Michigan that I can still scarcely believe even as I remember the stunning events unfold. The Sportscaster felt I was the only voice of reason at his new FM progressive rock station in Michigan. He decided to send me to Florida following a near mutiny which erupted during a meeting organized between the on air talent and Board members.

This extraordinary meeting was called to allow the Board to recognize the great success of the Sportscaster's new station. Ratings and revenue performance like this was unprecedented on FM radio coming into the 70's. The events unfolded just 1 year after Woodstock when most people didn't even have FM radio in their cars or homes as our station launched. Oh but when it launched it didn't just shine it dazzled, it quickly cornered the rock market consequently turning over incredible and unprecedented profits for its conservative shareholders.

Nonetheless the forum was called to order on this unforgettable meeting as an elegant elderly gent and designated spokesman for the Board on this day took the floor slowly warming to his subject. He ventured forth graciously into generous recognition of individual efforts and congratulated all staff on great radio along with remarkable results. Effusive lauds continued on the part of the Board recognizing individual contributions, rapid achievements, stellar financial success, radical new sounds, imagination, a creative new format, new music, the relaxed conversational approach to radio that listeners related fulsomely to and which had clinched the lead position on FM, and, and...and.

Individual disc jockeys were singled out for recognition then given glowing and generous tributes, likewise unique writing and innovative production for their merits and so on. Having found his words resonating with his audience (all of whom met the Board uniformly dressed in jeans and T-shirts) he continued boldly with a dissertation commending to them his personal vision for the future of FM.

He was quickly shut down by an "on air announcer" who eloquently set forth with his own urgent agenda and rapidly fired back, "If you're so proud of our success, why aren't we being properly compensated? If you appreciate our radical approach so much why not learn more about us, our attitudes, our goals and what radio means to us, or what our vision is for the future of FM?"

This young on air talent now drunk with confidence at finding his voice finally threw caution to the wind with, "Do you know that we get high every day to achieve the edgy radio that you like so much?" With his next utterance however even he knew he'd overstepped, "Do you know that most of us are high right now?" He continued on bravely as he threw down the gauntlet with, "In fact, in order to continue down this financially lucrative path there are some things we need you to approve, dude!"

1. "We cannot operate in the same building as the AM station. We can't be around the negative vibes coming from those announcers, news people, and office staff."

2. "You hired a black woman as the Traffic Director and we think that's great but she's the wrong black person dude, she's too old and too straight. We want to hire our own people."

3. "We need a house for new studios. We want to live and work together as a family unit."

4. "Finally, now that you know that we're all smoking pot for inspiration, we submit to you that you should underwrite its purchase as an essential part of doing business."

Looking around the room I watched the men in their impeccable suits balk, squirm and finally bristle with agitation. They nervously adjusted ties, tugged cuffs, eased collars while generally looking stunned and outraged. They called a halt to the meeting forthwith.

Within hours, everyone but Doc, the quiet and sensible one, was fired. Days later the station became "Stereo Island … music to help you escape." Huh? Like everywhere else across the country at this time society was truly at a crossroads. The runaway express train that was the voice of youth which had trickled into the culture in the late 60's was suddenly an unstoppable juggernaut. Generations clashed and drifted apart, fracturing and sliding in opposite directions.

Shortly after the fallout from this infamous but no less seminal board meeting and with Stereo Island mellifluously wafting melancholy across the airwaves like a malignancy, I was offered a job in Florida. It paid $250 a week and offered great potential for advancement, all because I was seen as having stood out among the crowd in that infamous meeting.

"Others," the Sportscaster pressed forth with his withering diatribe even many years later as we'd reminisce about that extraordinary meeting "were hell bent on destruction like a bunch of bums!" The Sportscaster really wanted me to go to Florida. He said he'd talked to the Jazzman and both had agreed I should move there to start fresh and as importantly to them away from those bum hooligans in Detroit.

I felt this was a very special calling and rushed at the chance to move to Florida eager to earn half of the money I was making in Detroit. I talked with the Jazzman only once before the move. He told me that in addition to the base salary I could earn up to $150 more a week as a DJ at clubs. He wanted me to be there in two weeks. He said he'd pay for a U-Haul, gas, and put me up in a hotel on the beach until I found my feet. I was young but I also recognized some special but still nonspecific opportunity that may flow from this next junction in my life.

I'd just arrived in Ft. Lauderdale with belongings in tow. I quickly dumped everything in my room and prepared for my first meeting with the Jazzman which was scheduled in the lobby of my beach-side hotel. He drove up in a long, sleek, gold colored Oldsmobile Tornado. He'd left home that morning it was transparently obvious to me with the express intention of capturing at least his quotient of attention. Showmanship was part and parcel of his charm.

He was a vision. He looked magnificent as he arrived to pick me up. He was wearing a red jacket with brass buttons, white pants and white lace up leather loafers. He elegantly smoked a long, decadent and not surprisingly expensive Cuban cigar. He certainly got attention; all eyes were transfixed by this ostentatious man around town. He really was quite a sight with shoulder length salt and pepper hair and full mutton chops. He reminded me of a resplendent peacock in full regalia. At three-hundred pounds he looked like a pinch of the circus that had broken loose though when he got out of his car I quickly noted that despite his size he had strong athletic moves. He was flashy but surprisingly smart looking.

For years I started every day in the Jazzman's office. We were friends, confidants, mentor and apprentice, and were bonded as closely as father and son could be though we were new friends. He wanted to teach me everything he knew about business and discuss ways I might help with his eldest son.

Jazzman!

Thus, my first morning with the Jazzman was spent driving around Ft. Lauderdale in his gold limo. I was wearing a light grey, light weight, double-breasted suit. We must have looked like front men for Bill Cody's Wild West Show. No matter, the Jazzman liked me and I liked him. We drove around all the sights, mostly the beach areas, eventually we stopped and had lunch, talked about sports, his career, my career and finally his family. He seemed most wistful when he spoke about the problems he was experiencing with his eldest son. I was a positive influence on his son, Jazzman confided years later. I was there to bring calm to the neighborhood.

Finally we got to Jazzman's house around 2 p.m. It was a nice spot on a canal just off the Intra-coastal Waterway. He poured drinks which we took with us as we wandered out back to see his boat. We eventually returned inside and I found a place on a sofa. Jazzman went to the bedroom to wake his son.

THE JUDGE!

About 20 minutes later, an enormous young man stumbled from the hallway. He gathered his balance and walked slowly past me, his head cocked cagily as he looked me over through his unruly mop of long black hair that fell into his face. He grunted, continuing on his way out to the kitchen where he took a swig of cold milk from the refrigerator. I would see this routine again hundreds of times over many years. We had many long nights of Wild Turkey, nose candy, a joint or two, conversations interspersed with the obligatory shriek of "rock 'n' roll," a few hours of sleep around dawn then greet the new day ("Under no circumstances before 2 p.m. dude!") with that lusty swig of cold milk.

He was the evening DJ on Jazzman's AM station he told me. He asked if I wanted to go to the studios with him that night. We stopped by my hotel on the way so I could lose the suit then an hour later we were driving up and down the rows of an orange grove about 5 minutes from the station at over 100 mph. His car was a black, sleek, shiny GTO JUDGE. His radio persona was "The Judge" as well. It was apparent to me that the wild ride we were on was clearly intended to mark the Judge's supremacy over his domain and for the moment this apparently included me.

I knew the Judge liked me and he knew I knew it and our friendship was immediate. I recognized as did he that with my presence he'd finally have a real chance of convincing his father to allow him to launch a progressive rock format on the FM station. Look out!

Our differing opinions on style and content were sometimes just down-right comical and sometimes instructive but they none the less played out more than anyone imagined. He was a Michigan rock 'n' roller, while I was a southerner before there was southern rock. He loved Mitch Ryder, I loved the Temptations. He had been to MC5 concerts while I'd been on stage with the Beatles. He'd talk about Alice Cooper and I'd tell him about Ray Charles at the Royal Peacock in Atlanta on Sunday afternoons (the day for whites in the club). He loved Grand Funk, I liked Otis Redding. My favorite comics were Murray Roman and Lord Buckley, his Rodney Dangerfield and George Carlin.

We both loved Elvis, and although the cultural divide between us may have seemed vast the Judge and I were inseparable over many years. We were frat brothers with lots of cash. We were brash and necessarily brandished power to achieve our ends. Watch out world cause we were on a tear – anxious to make our mark on the world.

The Judge didn't want to live past 30, famously saying "Dude, living past 30 and getting old - how embarrassing walking around the world an old man." He was a scratch golfer and I was his friend. We drank Wild Turkey with a "girl" on the side, a St. Pauli Girl was his beer of choice.

Since we didn't want to waste drinking time explaining why we each wanted 11 shots of Wild Turkey, we had signs made and thereafter arrived at bars with signs we'd had made then we'd obligingly hold them up for bartenders as we entered, "11 shots of Wild Turkey, a girl on the side!" It made perfect sense that we should order exactly 11 shots since that was the number of players on a football team. Frat brother antics don't stop when you leave school, they just become more grandiose.

Here We Go!

Doc and the Judge were two sharp, young guns with savvy; they'd made lots of money for the men in suits who were behind them. They made more than enough for themselves, too, though for them it was never about money, it was simply about being dudes. The time had come. They blazed onto the scene leaving their legacy over a tumultuous decade.

By their parents' standards they were undeniably and certifiably fucked up. Friends agreed too but they also knew they were razor smart to boot! "Crazy like a fox both those boys are," allies and competitors alike would say. As their legend spread they began to add, "Everyone knows they're like a fox pack, they're shrewd, cunning, focused. They'll have you for breakfast - you know the type I mean?" I think the Judge saw it more as "Butch and the Kid."

Doc as a young Marine ...
"Road guards out!"

There was no hippie rhetoric, nor any peace or love medallions to be found here. Doc was a recently returned Marine. The Judge was a myopic, dyslexic, long-haired, sardonic, scratch-golfer, a lefty who played from the right side. Both misfits perhaps but it was 1970 and a lifelong friendship blossomed the night of Doc and the Judge's first meeting as they sat on the roof of the radio station. They were smoking. And they had two six-packs of St. Pauli Girl and a bottle of Wild Turkey.

Doc waited for the right moment to pour out with onerous gravity and equally weighted eloquence his thoughts with the Judge… "We'll never again be what we were yesterday and tomorrow not what we are today." The Judge chided, "That's heavy dude, toss me a girl." He hit it once then threw it all the way back, then asked for the bottle. Two shots of Wild Turkey and he finished with a jowl shaking, belch, followed by his own articulation on the matter, "Someday that thin thread that connects us to reality is going to snap!" I tossed him his Kool's.

So began a chaotic and precious friendship, the fundamentals of which were laid down that evening. They each agreed they were pretty fucked up, but it was sorted out and agreed that Doc would play the role of visionary, thinker, man of judgment and deal maker. The Judge was forever the brilliant flame of idealism that shone radiant.

The Wedding

The Judge got one of his abiding fantasies out of the way with unusual expediency even for him. He wanted to marry a tall bartender with big tits who loved the Dolphins, the Gators, the University of Michigan, Notre Dame Football, Arnold Palmer, and Muhammad Ali. No mean feat I'm sure you'd agree.

Needless to say the Judge had his pick of bartenders and cocktail waitresses. He never left a tip of less than $50 and if the bill was more than $100 then the tip equaled the tab. I remember on one particular occasion giving the Judge $125 as the tip for a $125 dollar tab. He hated small denominations and so he'd asked me to get the five twenty dollar notes changed for a hundred dollar bill, then to add $25 to the remaining $25 to make it total $50.00. He felt that the $100 and $50 bills together would be more impressive than lots of smaller notes with the bar staff.

To this end I asked our waitress to make the exchanges, first she took the five twenty's to the cashier and traded them for a hundred dollar bill which she brought back to us, then I gave her $50 in various denominations and asked her to bring back a $50 bill. As we prepared to leave the bar we'd ask if we'd been "good customers?" The answer was always, "yes!" We always asked if she'd served, "customers quite like us?" The answer was always, "uh uh, no." Finally the carrot was dangled with the Judge holding up the $150 asking if this bought us extra favors. The answer was mostly, "well, maybe, but not much." Then he'd hold up another fifty and ask for a phone number and when we might call. The response was generally, "Great, call me tonight." That was how Doc and the Judge on occasion developed plans for the evening.

It was a fateful night when a short bartender with huge tits got the nod from the Judge. The scene was electric, and had the "ring of perfect for a day or two" authenticity about it. In short it was every fairy tale rolled into one only this tale starred an all drinking, all snorting, big tit, princess with salty vocabulary winning this valiant prince's heart. When we got to her apartment, we met her roomy who had small tits. They were twins.

I was bored and thereby asleep in minutes to the rhythm of love coming from the other room. The amorous couple locked themselves up for a love-in rivaled only by John Lennon and Yoko Ono's for a few days. After this magical period ended the Judge left the apartment to call me with genuine urgency in his tone sharing his powerful conviction that, "This short, big tit, bartender is the one dude."

We arranged to meet at a bar to discuss his latest need - an emergency wedding! "Why this one Judge," I asked. "She fits," he said, "anyway, I like the way she says "fuck me, fuck me, fuck me." "Judge come on, you know they all say that," was the most intellectual guidance I could offer on the spot. I shared information with him gleaned back in school in Georgia where couples routinely headed to South Carolina to secure emergency marriages - in a day! In Georgia this was usually done to save the young lady's virtue and the young man's hide. We synchronized watches and arranged to gather at a set time to leave for South Carolina that evening.

The Judge and the buxom bride were married at 4 p.m. at the Courthouse in Aiken, South Carolina the next day. Naturally as the only other party to this affair I tripled as Best Man, photographer and signatory to the proceedings. The Best Man's obligations now dispensed with I offered up a hasty toast to the newlyweds then suggested we hit the road for Atlanta to catch Brother Dave Gardner at the Domino Lounge where we'd celebrate the adorable couple with some good southern humor. Everybody agreed so off we went.

His bride whispered she'd been experiencing an increasingly urgent "call of nature" and needed a bathroom "NOW" just as we entered a two-lane country road. "Must be nerves," she offered with anguish. I slowed the car and started pulling over safely out of traffic, whereupon she took off for some bushes before the car had fully stopped. She scooped up her dress and began running wildly toward some bushes ahead.

The moment we lost sight of her we heard an unusual plop sound, and thereafter her cries coming from beyond the bushes, quickly followed by laughter, then endless, "fuck me, fuck me dead, fuck meee." In a few minutes she emerged to let us know she'd run straight into an open cesspool and immediately sank to her waist in her white wedding dress and her killer white satin bridal sandals. It was indeed, "A nice day for a white wedding" two full decades before Billy Idol's immortal anthem.

She cursed, moaned, screamed and cried as she made her way back to the car. Every step of hers toward the car led the Judge to take several corresponding steps back from the steaming, stinking slime that covered her from head to toe in the still afternoon heat that was summertime in Georgia. The Judge added with humor and disgust, "Honey, we just got married and offered our vows before God, which included richer and poorer, better or worse…sickness and health, not shitty and stinky! Sorry babe but you're walking." She appeared to be in total shock.

The Judge asked me how far we were from the next town. When I answered a couple of miles, he reiterated just in case there was any confusion that she'd definitely be walking. She walked in a daze by the car still wildly crying, screaming, cursing but interspersed now with shrill peals of laughter in utter disbelief at her predicament. Finally she was able to flag down a pickup truck and the driver allowed her to ride in the back. Just like in the movies she told him to, "Step on it and follow the car in front."

When we arrived in town I walked toward the driver and attempted to offer him a tip for his assistance. He seemed to be a rather typical shy and retiring old southern gent. While he flatly refused and suggested I was, "very generous" the incident had in fact made his day. "Anyway," he added, "it don't seem right to accept money from a couple of newlyweds getting off to such a shitty start," chortling heartily at his own excellent humor. All in all, his Georgia humor was a great appetizer for Brother Dave.

We hosed the Judge's new bride down at the fire house in town; she changed into jeans further along at a gas station. In Atlanta, the Judge bought his new bride a fancy black, low cut dress. Brother Dave introduced her on stage that evening as a big-tit, Ft. Lauderdale bartender who'd chosen to spend her wedding night with him. I have no notion what happened in those next two days, nor in fact how we got back to Florida safely.

Back home, the Judge's first purchase as a family man was a Siberian husky he named "Shit-ka." He wanted to get on with the full family experience. He went on to explain he wanted to begin the marriage steeped in tradition like others do. So despite buying the gorgeous puppy all the way in Sitka, Alaska he felt naming it Shit-ka more appropriately honored his wedding day memories.

Sadly, the marriage didn't last, though there was a collective twitter of shock among friends, all stunned that the marriage had lasted quite as long as it had. We heard the collective clucking and drawing of breath in awe as they cited it may have lasted as many as several weeks, can you imagine it? They chortled in chorus.

Nonetheless, the Judge and his short, big tit, Venus were enlightened pragmatists and remained firm friends and drinking buddies. They understood the kindred spirit concept and quickly acknowledged that for them beyond drinking, sex, and having fun they had nothing at all in common.

This predicament was no one's fault it simply failed to live up to the fantasy. Apparently she wanted a man she could control. As for his part the Judge knew he could rely on the Doc for a strong shoulder to laugh on. He moved on quickly in high dudgeon.

Doc and the Judge set forth on new adventures, the Judge still laughing heartily at this lucky escape. The Judge's real fantasy was to take over the Jazzman's FM radio station. He wanted an outlet to express what was in his head: straight ahead rock 'n' roll, free expression, zero bullshit, all envisioned through the prism of a chaotic, savant, young mind. He got his wish and thus "SHE" was born. WSHE ... "She's only rock 'n' roll bitch," the Judge would say with a hiss.

Flying High

Jazzman wanted us to fully understand the workings of radio ratings. To this end, twice a year he'd send us to the Arbitron ratings headquarters in Maryland to scour the data and gloat gleefully at our own success. We always upgraded the purchase of his coach tickets to first class. In first class we could get drinks before the plane took off and the service along the way was more to our liking.

On this particular trip we flew into Baltimore a night early so we could catch girls on stage at one of the dives on the Baltimore Strip. On the way to Arbitron the following morning we stopped and bought a six pack of "girls," we liked to bury them in the snow and sneak away during breaks and throw back a cold one.

We timed our visit one year so we could stop over in Atlanta on the return trip to Florida to catch an Atlanta Falcons football game. The Judge looked like Alice Cooper and on this particular occasion after getting a radical micro haircut myself topped off with oversized sunglasses I passed for Elton John.

About halfway thru the flight, the attendant leaned over us conspiratorially asking if we're someone important? The Judge responded wincingly at the apparent pain of recognition then placing his finger to his lip he whispered in a pleading voice, "People call me Alice, my friend's last name is John but please respect our privacy, we're on our way to Miami for a recording session after a stopover so he can catch his first American football game." Well, as you might imagine all hell broke loose!

The standard Delta champagne glasses were immediately replaced by crystal flutes, next the attendant stopped by again this time urging us to visit the captain in the cockpit. I cautioned, "I don't like this Judge, you know I can't pull off a British accent!" He told me not to speak just nod yes or no to all questions. He told the attendant I had laryngitis and had been ordered by an ENT specialist to rest my voice. He then made it clear he however had no such restrictions to worry him and would be delighted to meet with the pilot. He sat like a joyous child in the co-pilot's seat for some time, he was asked to autograph what he suspected was the flight log.

Later, the attendant came alerting us to the fact that people in coach had heard we were on board (which she confirmed no doubt), now they'd implored her to prevail upon us to wander back to coach and oblige them with a meet and greet. So, with one attendant leading the way and one protecting our rear end we walked back and forth through coach.

We'd occasionally stop, arbitrarily point to passengers to whom the girls would offer beverages compliments of Alice and Elton. I heard whispers of, "that's not them," which was quickly followed by, "yes it is and I should know I have all their albums and I've seen them in concert!" To our horror this misery was to endure even after touchdown. Word got to us that the captain had helpfully alerted Atlanta that Alice Cooper and Elton John were on board, which meant we should expect paparazzi to greet us upon arrival.

Think fast, Doc. Ok, I think I've developed a workable, plausible plan. I'd sneak off the plane immediately and swap our scheduled rental car for a limo. We'd arrange for our driver to retrieve our luggage and we'd bail out of the airport post haste. I told the Judge to hide in a bathroom, wait for my signal to come out then we'd wait until all the luggage had been claimed but our own.

We set in place our plan, so, as planned the driver grabbed our luggage then we bolted out of there toward the limo before the shit hit the proverbial fan! The plan was flawless and worked perfectly, almost!

We were on our last strides to the limo when I was approached by a very elegant business executive. He approached nervously, his left arm in a cast and said, "Mr. John? My daughter loves you and she'd never forgive me if I didn't at least attempt to get your autograph for her." My heart was racing and my instinct whispered "don't sign" but I felt for this lone man in the parking lot advocating for his daughter. I could see my mother's heart heavy at the deception however on balance I passed both the Kantian and Utilitarian threshold morally by signing as my intention was pure. Many were helped at that moment and no-one hurt, I scrawled "Best, Elton" scurrying for sanctuary into the limo.

I still wonder what happened to that cast. Is it still out there keeping pride of place that some middle aged housewife proudly shares with friends and family telling of her father's fabulous story of stealth the evening he got Elton's autograph.

Or perhaps it's long since been sold on eBay for a tidy sum of money? As we drove away, one lone TV cameraman filmed the departing limo. Is it sitting in a vault like a ticking time bomb reminiscent of Zapruda's chronicle documenting John Kennedy's assassination?

Oh what a night!

Ladies and Gentlemen, Doc and the Judge Have Left Memphis

A prominent music/radio publication had recently relocated from Los Angeles and the Judge and I were invited to the grand opening of its new headquarters in Memphis. An equally compelling reason to take the trip was that the Judge heard that we'd likely have snow in Memphis; he was beside himself at the prospect of snow. We got to the party then ditched it in record time upon finding the same old clapped out hags with the same old withering stories full of the same old self congratulatory rhetoric.

We were under siege from mindless top-40 disc jockeys leading the Judge to quip, "Dude, they're more plastic than those straws making the rounds along with that white powder." No matter, we had far more dazzling plans.

We wanted to see Beale Street. We wanted to find and drink in the bars Elvis had hung out in with the Memphis Mafia. We struck up a conversation with a local homeless man. It was apparent he'd been born here, had spent all his life here, and would surely die here too.

We asked about the origin of the name Beale Street? He said, "A long time ago boys we lived way over there, but people who owned our houses lived over here. Every Friday we would come here to pay our 'beels' thus it became Beale Street for us, then transferred into folklore after a time." History shows that Beale Street was actually named after a forgotten civil war hero but the local's adaptation is far more colorful.

I asked how he felt about Martin Luther King being killed in his city. He said, "He knew he was going to be killed; we are honored that his memory will always be linked to Memphis." He then broke into an eloquent recitation of Shakespeare. Huh? Another one of those surprising American tales, perhaps he was a thespian in another life before the booze took him down. We asked if there was anything we could do for him. He answered, "A taste of vodka would be good." We followed his lead to a liquor store and told him to take his pick of brand and make it a large bottle. He went back to the streets holding a bottle of what I think was Stoli, the new vodka of choice, under his arm.

The Judge had undergone two unsuccessful cornea transplant surgeries. His eyesight continued to deteriorate which obviously upset him, though on the upside he crowed, "Dude I'll buy and wear a black leather eye patch over my bad eye." He'd persuaded himself immediately then endlessly tried to persuade me, "Don't you see how cool it is?" "Yes, it lends you gravitas dude," I thought to myself. A seductive mystery if you will. His was the real king of bling many decades before Diddy or other gangsta rappers.

His surgeries were performed by a Ft. Lauderdale doctor of some notoriety, a former Marine Captain no less who as a medical student volunteered to participate in Timothy Leary's experiments with LSD. He boasted he'd run in the Boston Marathon every year, bragging he'd done all 26 miles on acid and everyone who knew him believed him. He experimented with marijuana-laced brownies that he served to unsuspecting glaucoma patients, mostly aging silver haired dowagers from the north seeking treatment. A government grant was given for experimentation with liquid cocaine eye drops again to bring relief for glaucoma. The man had found his niche and was in his element. The Judge and I always felt this authorized study grant was akin to making Dracula CEO of the blood bank.

Needless to say the good doctor was extremely popular around Ft. Lauderdale's bars where he always arrived with a nasal spray full of this heady potion. There was a memorable place in Ft Lauderdale that had a running toy train along the length of the bar delivering drink orders to patrons. He'd slip his nasal spray on the train's carriage stopping it in front of select people perched around the bar. He also was known as the "lude" dude. He favored friends with endless scripts of 714's. The Judge took a few of the pills with him for the Memphis trip.

Like clockwork, we knew that the Judge would feel the effects of the "lude" exactly 30 seconds after I did. He would look at his watch with his one good eye ready to time it when I told him I was "there." On this night in Memphis I eventually convinced the Judge we ought to head back to the hotel and attempt to get some sleep before we got into any trouble. When we reached our room I promptly fell asleep only to be woken in what seemed like minutes with the Judge jumping up and down on my bed like an excited three-year-old screaming "wake up.....it's snowing dude."

We got dressed and decided to walk down the street through the snow to a bar located across a freeway overpass from our hotel. When we got downstairs and into the cold night air we quickly discovered we couldn't walk straight. Quite inexplicably however we found we could run straight without any problem at all, so we ran wildly, delighting in the white magic surrounding us. As usual this proved to be a very poor decision indeed.

We ran right into the lobby with the Judge unable to stop running and so barreling straight into the hotel's Christmas tree knocking it over along with the painstakingly placed decorations adorning it ever so graciously for the genteel clientele. People scrambled to pick the Judge up off the floor. I heard murmurings that police be called.

I told the Judge not to worry. I assured him I'd find the hotel manager and explain everything including the rather tall tale that my friend was on drugs following very recent eye surgery. I'd implore him to be reasonable as I explained my friend lost his balance as we ran into the venue to get in from the outside blizzard we were eager to get in out of. I felt a deep conviction in my plan saving him I assured the Judge.

I had the manager pointed out to me by staff; he was having dinner with friends in the dining room. Quite inexplicably as I approached his table ready to explain my friend's predicament, I tripped on the carpet, stumbled then fell straight into their table. In a momentary sense of slow motion, I was conscious of spilling everyone's hearty winter soup into every lap at the table as it lurched back and forth.

I pleadingly apologized to the manager in particular and the table in general now for both the Judge's behavior and the Doc's. I begged his forgiveness and indulgence while bravely continuing with my story. The manager stood up and said, "Son, I'm very sorry to hear about your friend, of course we understand and naturally your friend can stay. You on the other hand have to leave... Now!" There was a sheriff and swarm of backup police there in what seemed like mere minutes.

After a brief look around at the fracas along with some cursory discussions with witnesses, the deputy approached us then quipped, "Boys the way I see it, you have two choices. Leave Memphis on the next plane, or go to Memphis jail otherwise referred to as hell - your choice!" We promised that we would be on the first flight out.

Sitting glumly in first class as the plane taxied the runway the Judge saw I was unusually glum, he asked, "Dude, what's wrong? This ain't like you Doc." I told him that what happened last night rattled me. I said, "It's the closest call I've ever had with the law, besides I'm at a loss as to how I can explain this to Jazzman …"

For a few minutes we sat quietly with the blinding sun shining through the plane's oval windows then the Judge looked at me hissing, "Don't be upset Doc, why the hell would we ever want to come back to Memphis anyway. We came here, did what we wanted to do, and left our mark." He then rubbed his right hand across his forehead, which was his way of saying that I should erase it from my mind.

Rock 'n' roll!

The Judge is Arrested

By now the Judge had lost the privilege of driving for repeat speeding infractions in his beloved Judge! Sadly, every cop in Ft. Lauderdale knew the car, the driver and of the driver's eccentric driving. So, on the rare occasion I wasn't available to drive the Judge, he'd turn to others. One particular night the Judge and the Elf (a nickname given to a person who served as a music intern for the Judge) were meeting some record reps in a local bar. The reps left early and so the Judge and the Elf stayed on continuing to drink. A fight broke out with the two of them being hurled across a table by a couple of guys who were pissed off that their dates had taken an irritating interest in them.

I received a phone call very late that night advising me the Judge and the Elf were in the Ft. Lauderdale jail and wanted me to come down and organize bail. When I arrived I heard the deafening clank, clank, clank of metal on metal akin to a drinking cup being dragged back and forth across the steel bars. I heard a voice screaming, "Get me out of here," which I thought was overkill as they'd been locked up under an hour.

None the less, I posted bail and waited for these "ne'er do wells" to emerge. The door opened and the Elf rushed into my arms hugging me, reminiscent of a Hollywood romantic scene missing only the soaring symphonic music to set the appropriate mood. My gaze was fixed expectantly over his shoulder waiting for the Judge to emerge.

In short order however the guard let me know that though Mr. Elf would be leaving with me, Mr. Judge wished not to be disturbed. He added helpfully "Sir, Mr. Judge wishes not to be disturbed. He'd like to get a good night's rest, but he says he'd appreciate it if you'd be good enough to return tomorrow to collect him." Huh, was this the Sheriff or his "man servant?"

Jailhouse Rock!

Doc and the Judge

The Joker and Another Arrest

Steve Miller's *Joker* album was released just as the Judge and I were scheduled to leave for Atlanta to get to a Lynyrd Skynyrd concert. We'd been sent Steve Miller *Joker* masks by their record company reps prior to the trip. Ill advised you may think, in fact tick a big yes in that box. Nonetheless we threw caution and good judgment to the wind and set out wearing those masks everywhere and all the time on this fateful trip.

We wore the masks on the plane, even asking for straws so we might continue sipping our adult beverages through the mask's mouth opening. Naturally there was never any likelihood of bothering with the meals offered on board so the masks never presented any problems there.

An elderly first class traveler was waiting by the bathroom and peed all over himself disturbed and shocked by the Judge, all six foot four of him as he exited the lavatory wearing a full mask. The gentleman ran from the bathroom waiting area arms flailing about him and urine running down his suit pants with the telltale trickle all along the corridor back to his now very moist seat. We wore the masks throughout the cab ride into Atlanta and continued to wear them as we checked into the hotel. We planned to wear them to the Falcon's football game the following day. The next morning in Underground Atlanta we knew the masks would get lots of attention in the crowd so wearing them was both a given and a firm commitment to our antics.

We had just stepped out of the cab to start our walk toward the entrance when we were promptly stopped by a couple of policemen who were quickly backed up by several more support squads and then more policemen on horseback. We were thrown against the wall and patted down.

They began dragging us away and we got very nervous about the overly zealous response and in an attempt to explain we asked if they'd heard of the Steve Miller Band? One of the cops said yes easing back his grip on our handcuffs. We explained that we were part of the Steve Miller promotion for his newly released album *The Joker*, which is why we were wearing the masks. Quite unbelievably we learned from these policemen that there had been a spate of robberies in Atlanta, including this specific area of the Underground where we were arrested, by two young men wearing masks.

Thank God for the rock 'n' roll brotherhood.

Unexpected Visit to the White House

We're on a long flight from Los Angeles where the Judge and I had gone to present a band that we absolutely felt sure would be picked up by a label. Along the way we decided to take a side trip to Washington, DC to see the Redskins play. A friend of Jazzman's from his Philadelphia time was a coach with the Redskins, an assistant coach for George Allen. Jazzman arranged for us to spend the night with the coach since the Judge was just a child the last time they'd seen each other.

Suddenly, there was a problem. The Judge and I both took a liking to a very tall and strikingly beautiful black flight attendant who was assigned in first class on this trip across country. She was incredibly voluptuous and for her part she later said she found us to be "refreshingly different." Yep, we were different.

She agreed to meet outside the Dulles terminal and spend some time showing us around her town. We were going to start by having aperitifs at a very famous and fashionably exclusive open bar overlooking the White House to wind down from the long arduous flight.

Two things had to be done upon our arrival in Washington. First I'd upgrade our rental car to a Lincoln Towne car for our improved prospects for our evening on the town. The second was the Judge would call the coach to say we couldn't make it to his house due to unexpected delays.

I drove the Lincoln out of the airport with the three of us in the front seat. She was carrying coke which she laid out on the dashboard at a stop sign. She was quickly animated and by the time we reached the general area of the White House and began negotiating unfamiliar streets her sharp, urgent directions of right, left stop instructions were coming thick and fast.

Then she yelled, "Stop now, stop, we've missed our turn." I quickly and I thought helpfully turned into the first driveway we came upon to remove myself from oncoming traffic and unwittingly straight into the private drive of 1600 Pennsylvania Avenue, promptly bumping into the gates of the White House.

Instant fear and shock turned into shrill peals of laughter at our own "Guess who's coming to dinner" moment, made even funnier no doubt after our earlier indulgence on the car's dashboard.

I slowly backed out of the driveway then a blinding moment followed as flood lights were turned onto us from the guardhouse. In short order guards with rifles were running toward us as, other backup officers follow right behind them should the situation require it.

For our part we continued to squeal like school girls despite the peril we felt sure we were in. There's nothing like a heightened emotional state to send you into apoplectic spasms of tears or as in our case irrepressible giggling through utter panic. When we caught sight of the military tour de force approaching us armed, angry and defensive we panicked and roared away quickly making turns anywhere the road permitted which quite unbelievably ended quietly at the bar she had wanted to take us to all along. The three of us sat on the veranda overlooking the White House enjoying the view and secretly looking over our shoulders for the rest of the evening to assure ourselves we hadn't been followed.

We loved that girl and loved her, and loved her and she loved us right back again and again. She missed her next flight and we missed the Redskins game. Oh what a night! The Judge and I talked about her for years. He never saw her again. I saw her once miraculously and as fate would have it I was traveling out of San Francisco with a female companion. There she was, imagine.

She said, "Hello Doc, I remember you and I'm proud to serve you on your flight back home." What followed was a series of "get evens" starting with wrong drinks served, cold dinners, followed by contact numbers slipped for lines long disconnected and so on. I'm still unsure if she was pissed off, overworked or simply irritable on the day? I guess I'll never know.

She's only rock 'n' roll and I like it.

Frat Brother Humor

A sales person's primary responsibility is to understand and solve the problems, issues or needs of their customers. Record reps in the 70's knew about our likes and dislikes and how we liked to spend our leisure time. A rep we called Glitch learned from the Judge that I liked deep-sea fishing. When I picked up the Judge that morning for the drive down to the marina, I spotted a dead bird on the ground en route and not knowing exactly what do with it, I wrapped it a bag and threw it in my cooler to bury at home.

There are 3 sharks in this picture. Count 'em.

The record rep began to feel a little queasy as the boat rollicked on the constant waves at sea. We were obliging and always striving to be helpful and so like a boy scout I knew what to do. I put some mayonnaise between two slices of bread and lay the little bird in the middle. When it was clear our friend was becoming violently sea sick, I told him not to worry and that I had the perfect cure, I assured him when I felt sea sickness coming on nothing was more helpful and settling than some food in one's stomach and to this end I prepared a quick sandwich for him.

I gave him the sandwich which he bit into immediately. I can still hear the crackling of the little bones and see feathers falling from his lips and dancing softly in the breeze. He was instantly ill ordering the boat's captain to take us back to shore.

He was pallid by now, clammy to the touch and had developed a grey hue to his skin. He asked that his wife be radioed to meet him at the dock. Only we knew what he had eaten; in his sickness he didn't know that he had bitten into a dead bird sandwich. The Judge is laughing.

Fly pretty bird, fly!

Handcuffs for Pretty Boy

And then there was the brilliant new star dazzling brilliantly and reigning supreme over the record industry. He's young, smooth, charismatic and charming, he's debonair and heartbreakingly handsome, he's a good southern boy who's fast tracked into the big time and he loves Doc and the Judge.

On the day he left for Los Angeles to take over a legendary record label, he asked if the Judge could score some Ritalin for him. He felt certain it would give him the extra confidence lift he'd need to hit La La Land and the big time by storm.

He'd also bought a brand new, baby blue, Mercedes Benz and arranged to meet us in the parking lot of the radio station to say goodbye on his way to Hollywood along with his bottle of confidence. The Judge always called him "Pretty Boy."

There was a record industry convention and it was to have the distinction of being the first convention held at the new and still incomplete Peachtree Plaza Hotel in Atlanta. The Judge and I recognized an opportunity for some mischief and mayhem for the astral travelling drugged up guests of this auspicious gathering. We conspired to mix up all the signs marking the floor numbers which had been placed that day and had not yet set permanently. We began by scattering the floor numbers at random.

It would be a huge challenge for these "high flyers" and this would be especially challenging toward the end of each evening by which time we knew the entire guest list was sky high. We wanted to test a theory, in short it was to establish how many if any of the self-proclaimed free spirits at the convention could navigate their way back to their rooms unassisted.

We suspected very few and in record time we were proven right as many spent the night on the lobby furniture, or any lounge chairs to be found scattered about the hotel. As they gave up on finding their rooms they laid claim to a sleeping area and slept in the common areas on any manner of chair, chaise or sofa. It was spookily reminiscent of a sudden snow-in at Denver airport during a blizzard.

One guy, an accountant type for a west coast concert company, told us he'd never experienced Quaaludes. And voila, enter the Judge to settle his niggling curiosity. He helpfully told him "it's best to take two and chase it with a girl dude." As a precaution we asked for a key to his room.

An hour later it was apparent he'd never find his room alone so we got him there and put him to bed fully clothed. We then slipped into the foyer and rolled in an operating coke vending machine which we then laid in bed beside him. We plugged the unit into a power outlet and let him sleep off his bliss. Late the following morning we found him and he eagerly recounted waking up utterly disoriented beside his purring coke machine. He explained he felt he was standing and feeling parched he searched his pockets for change for a Coke. His confusion escalated as his difficulty ambulating showed him to be horizontal in bed and not in fact in front of a vending machine in situ.

He confessed to sitting for a long period and searching his mind to make sense of how the coke machine ended up in bed with him. He winked and chortled to us, "I know the ads proclaim 'coke is it' but this dudes, this is ridiculous!"

Word was floating around the convention that Pretty Boy's arrival was delayed due to flight problems. We knew that upon arrival he would be standing in the lobby greeting convention arrivals. We knew the trademark meet and greet, back slapping and cheek sucking of this style svengali. If not a corporate high flyer, he would have been a formidable politician I always thought. We caught his arrival in the lobby and so launched our exquisitely planned and deliciously executed coup de grace.

We'd found and commissioned a very hefty black woman outside the hotel who agreed to go along with our plan for a tidy sum. We'd already locked one side of a handcuff onto her wrist and she followed us closely as we mingled while making our way toward the lobby. She was the soul of discretion about the handcuff on her wrist and so we awaited Pretty Boy's arrival and the imminent hug fest, followed by a hearty back slap that was his trademark.

Naturally, he was the axis around whom a throng of adoring acolytes and a gaggle of pretty young women orbiting around him while hanging on his every word. We approached to shake his hand and as he forwarded his hand the Judge reached out and slapped the other side of our girl's handcuff to his wrist. We walked away leaving Pretty Boy to drag his new "friend" around for hours until someone could be found to cut the cuffs off.

Years later, Pretty Boy was shot dead upstairs in his beach-side home by a young but recently estranged girlfriend who had found him in bed with someone else. Doc always felt confident after his untimely death that he hadn't died but had simply moved on to a big satin vibrating bed in the sky.

What's Keeping Us Apart?

On the rare occasion the Judge didn't get the "pick of the litter" I'd be called in to mediate. I used a business technique taught to me by Jazzman, "What's keeping us apart?" Jazzman would say, "You can never resolve an issue until you truly know what it is. Many issues are surrounded and encrusted by the unknown, the real objections. You must dig deep, peel back the layers and get to the core; otherwise you're negotiating with yourself. Be confident that you've identified the real issue before you offer solutions."

We're in a bar in New Orleans and the Judge had already sent two drinks to a striking, tall, leggy girl with a pixie haircut sitting conspicuously alone across the room. Both drinks had been returned with a message of "thanks but no thanks." The Judge gives me his big cow eye and asks me to intervene. To this end I step in as master mediator.

I approached her with an ice breaking line, "Do you think both ways?" She responded with a blank face and, "What?" I immediately detected a deep southern accent even in this monosyllabic utterance. I offered graciously "Let me guess, you're from the south and I'd narrow it down specifically to Mississippi." She replies, "Now how on earth did you know that, in fact I'm from Greenville, Mississippi. You just guessed that didn't you?" "No, I replied. It's something I've mastered over the years," I said boldly plagiarizing a memorable line of Professor Dr. Henry Higgins from *My Fair Lady* who famously was able to detect accents from across England. As I now had her full attention and enthusiastic engagement I pressed on with, "Identifying where a person's from by the distinctive local color in their accent is what I do, in some cases I can actually guess what they do for a living as well."

I said to her, "See that guy and girl over there? I'll bet you he's a doctor, southerner, married, and that girl with him isn't his wife." "They're friends of yours, right," was her droll response. Using the old "sin of omission" technique, you know, giving a plausible answer without offering details about unasked questions, I said, "Look, we arrived very late last night then we slept most of the day and this here and now is our first time out, here in this bar. How could I possibly know that person?" I could tell by her expressive face it was working. I told her of my proposition. "Let's send them drinks, then walk over to their table and strike up a conversation. If I'm right, that he's a southern doctor, and she's his girlfriend, you'll agree to answer one question for me in return." How could she refuse this harmless proposition?

As we approached their table, I reached out to shake his hand and said, "Doctor, how are you?" I saw a dazed and confused look in his face. He asked "How did you know I was a doctor?" I said, "I can spot doctors a mile away, they call me Doc too." The conversation revealed that he was an orthopedic surgeon from Memphis, was in New Orleans with his girlfriend for the week-end. Naturally, he said nothing about his wife and two kids back home.

Mission accomplished. Back at her table, she said, 'How'd you do that, and you didn't tell me you were a doctor," to which I answered, "I didn't say I was a doctor, I said people call me Doc. Hello, I'm Doc, and you are?" "My name is Tammy. OK Doc, so you won the bet … now what's your question?"

I looked over at the Judge and held up two fingers signaling that we just fin-ished two quarters, halftime already and naturally the home team is winning. She wanted to know why I'd held up two fingers. "To order two more drinks," I said thinking fast on my feet. She was a perceptive little minx.

"And now Tammy for the question, see my friend over there, the tall one with a patch over his right eye. He's sent two drinks over to you both of which were returned." I saw the possibilities of where this conversation was leading ticking over in her brain, so I cut to the chase… "I'm here to ask you what's keeping you two apart? Be honest, you can give me up to three reasons."

She took a sip of a drink a waiter had just put down on the table for her. She started tentatively with her summation of the Judge "Well, first he looks like a rock 'n' roller, with his shirt open and his collar turned up and I don't like rock 'n' roll. Secondly, I don't like men with long hair and finally he looks like a pirate with that patch over his eye. He just looks scary."

I waited till she'd finished then said, "Is there anything else keeping you two apart, now's the time to speak up Tammy." She looked down at her drink and started again, "Look, there is one more thing, my friend Debbie's a flight attendant and she'll be here any minute. She's taking a layover in New Orleans and I drove down here from Greenville so we could have a weekend together." OK Doc, I quickly encapsulate the dilemma in this situation, she didn't like the way he's dressed, hates rock 'n' roll, is afraid of pirates, and her flight attendant friend will be here soon. Bingo, we can make this work, no problem. I knew it was in the bag.

I told her to sit tight, have another drink and said I needed a quick word with my friend that wouldn't take long at all and that I'd be right back. As I approached the Judge he was almost salivating like Pavlov's dogs with anticipation.

I offered up, "OK Judge, this should be fairly straight forward. Go upstairs and put on a fresh white shirt, while you're about it kill the gold necklace then put your hair in a ponytail and stuff it inside your baseball cap." Finally I suggested he leave the eye patch in the room. I added for good measure, "When I introduce you to her talk about country artists, in fact mention Charlie Daniels and I'm sure she'll be putty in your man hands dude." I then wound it up with, " Dude, her friend Debbie's a flight attendant and will be joining her shortly." I made my way back to the lovely southern elfin princess and told her he'd be right over.

Did it work? Of course, it always worked. We toured New Orleans in one of those horse driven carriages all night and we got real drunk. We were up so late we eventually saluted the sunrise, spent the next 24 hours in our respective rooms interrupted only by room service. Wink.

By the end of the first day she was stroking the Judge's long hair, walking around their room nude except for the Judge's disco shirt draped around her, and in some kind of psychological breakthrough proudly wearing his eye patch.

And what about her flight attendant friend I hear you ask. Well, it turned out she loved long walks, sitting on the balcony watching the nightly melee of tit-flashing on Bourbon Street below. She confessed a deep-seeded inquisitiveness of being in bed with another woman and two dudes. Whoa! Successful negotiating Doc, tick that box and highlight it. And Tammy told me later that she finally understood my opening line at the bar when I asked, "Do you think both ways?" Now, imagine that Tammy and Debbie went on to enjoy a happy lifetime relationship together. Matchmaker could be added to my long list of credentials.

How did I know about the doctor and his girlfriend? By the time the Judge and I got to the hotel bar the night before it was almost closing time. The only other person at the bar was a pitiful, self absorbed, young man who was at the end of at least 24 hours of heavy drinking and self indulgent naval gazing. He was ordering a tray of shooters in fear of the bar closing before he'd successfully drowned out every last demon inside him.

He slurred he was a doctor from Memphis, that he was the first in his family to graduate from college, that he didn't feel he deserved all the riches that life had blessed him with, that he'd slipped away for the weekend with a girl he barely knew, leaving his wife and two children at home. He slurred on that his girlfriend left him at the bar hours ago to go to bed, and that he was very lonely and needed another drink.

Well, we asked the bartender to call the hotel manager to escort this young doc back to his room. I knew that he would have absolutely no memory of the night before which is why I had no fear of approaching him and his girlfriend at their table with Tammy.

The Judge, a blonde, and Doc. So what's new!

So in conclusion class, here are three things to answer to graduate Cum Laud from the Doc of Love Academy:

1) Ask the question, "Do you think both ways?"
2) Seek to understand the delicate principle of, "Sin of omission."
3) Always ask, "What's keeping us apart?"

These tried and true tools worked flawlessly every time for Doc and the Judge. Oh, to have enjoyed the simplicity of the "do it dude" 70's. Tonight's homework is to test the theory, test and retest the theory to prove the theory. Class dismissed.

No Oral Dude - Just a Blow Job!

The Judge and I are relaxing at a beach bar known to be frequented by rich, middle aged women mostly from Michigan who sought the balmy tropical climes of Florida to escape the cold and their equally cold and boring husbands. These ladies lunched, shopped, and attempted to outdo each other with exploits with the multitude of young studs around the bars every evening.

On this night the Judge is getting eye-fucked from across the bar by a pleasantly attractive blond in her mid-forties; she's cool, elegant and is dressed in Saks and Neiman style. Without a word ever being spoken between them she slips across the room, takes the Judge by the hand and lures him with her. I'm sure he thought about it for a second and beat her to the rendezvous point.

As he left he turned to me winking, always powerfully, wickedly confident in his irresistibleness. For her part she turns to me and whispers breathlessly, "We'll be back soon, meantime you're drinking on my tab." The Judge whispers in my ear, "Wanna come dude?" To which I yawn lazily, "No thanks, you'll be back before your bar seat's cooled down, enjoy."

A half hour later I see him blindly navigating his way through the crowd back to the bar, his patch mockingly festooning his good eye. When he was close enough "Oral?" I asked. He offered helpfully, "No dude, no talking - just a very weird blow job!"

He continued, "This bitch had me standing naked in the ocean, while she tried to balance on her knees in the surf. It was weird, she deep-throated me then reached under and crushed my gonads. Shit dude, if I didn't know better I'd swear I'd been had by a pro."

He continued with his (excuse the pun) blow by blow account, "Doc, the weirdest thing was when I came, it literally blew off the wig she was wearing into the water!" He pressed on in nauseating detail, "And get this dude, she didn't skip a beat, she just swept it up out of the foam and used it to clean me up." I could see the experience was haunting him, he offered urgently, "Dude, look at me, I'm still shaking!"

"What's her name, where is she now?" I asked him. He retorted, "Who the hell knows, I just called her Maggie May. She told me she'd go to her room to clean up and change." In a pitch I'd only heard in the Judge's most vulnerable and anxious moments he added, "Dude she said she and her girlfriend would be down here in a few minutes and they'd take us sailing tomorrow." I quip "No thanks dude. There's only the quick and the dead and there's no time for niceties with sharks."

"No shit," he offered adding, "I don't want to see that face again, and certainly God forbid in broad daylight." He turned his attention to the bartender calling out, "Hey, two shots of Wild Turkey and two girls on the side, this is urgent."

He turned to me with panic overcoming him and hissed, "Doc, let's get the hell outta here dude!"

Oral fixation – huh?

Touched by a Hollywood Angel

We liked to schedule recording artists in Ft. Lauderdale for private Sunday afternoon concerts in venues about town. Most of those artists were not core to our station's music however these formats gave us a chance to do something out of the ordinary for our clients.

The groups in time came to showcase luminaries including Flip Wilson, Buddy Rich, Melissa Manchester and others. On one occasion the entertainment was a female singer/actress affectionately referred to as "Nostril-dame-us." After the show a private party was held at Jazzman's house by the pool on the canal. Nostril-dame-us left us with indelible, unforgettable memories.

Following 'Nostril-dame-us' performance we got to the party, and then asked her to join us across the street at Andy Granatelli's house. The legendary Indy 500 race car driver had become the TV spokesman of STP; he's the guy who'd stand in front of the camera wearing a trench coat holding up a can of STP as the race cars zoomed by in the background. Since Nostril-dame-us suggested she'd love to shoot pool, we went to Andy's game room where we'd play a game of 8-ball.

Unbeknown to us someone stepped up generously laying thick lines of cocaine the entire length of the pool table. Then our intrepid host Andy walks in. His reputation as a neat nut was universal; not surprisingly on this occasion seeing what he imagined to be chalk dust all over his table in front of guests he apologized, mumbled indulgently about the quality of help these days then quickly set to work with a hand held vacuum annihilating the imminent mountain of fun.

The unforgettable image of Nostril-dame-us' nostrils flaring larger than one could imagine possible as the candy disappeared is burned on my retina forever, she was inconsolable and left shortly thereafter for the limo ride back to the hotel…

Ridin That Train….

The Train Ride

The Judge and I decided to dive into the full Agatha Christie nostalgic experience of rail and so headed to Atlanta by unfashionable but elegant rail. There was an eager betting pool percolating with short odds being we wouldn't survive any further than the first hours without creature comforts and need for immediate gratification. The train boarded in Ft. Lauderdale maneuvering up the coast into Jacksonville where we'd board another service which would whisk us to Atlanta via Birmingham, Alabama.

When we boarded in Ft. Lauderdale the Judge slapped a hot $100 bill in the sweaty palms of the now deliriously happy attendant asking him to look after us. We had a sleeper but for the first few hours of the trip we were distracted and excited enough to spend our time soaking up the atmosphere in the club car.

In short order the Judge's roving eye for pretty babes zoomed in on a girl with that notorious bad eye. He was convinced she was Freda Payne - the young, black, up and coming singing star at the time. Although the Judge was disappointed to find the young babe was not in fact Freda, in record time he and the aforementioned hot babe adjourned to her room for a few sweaty hours.

He later joined me back in the sleeper with some new acquaintances for Wild Turkey and poker. Not long afterward I was declared the winner and everybody eventually scattered back to their own compartments. The Judge now rested and cooled down but seething at having lost a goodly deal of money adjourned to rejoin his hot babe to work off his current agitation in the only way that worked for him, live, hot and sweaty, sweet thang action.

We were coasting uneventfully just north of Orlando, and I'm back in my bunk by now preparing to step onto the floor to make a bathroom stop. Just as I took my first unsteady step to the floor the train jerked violently and I utterly lost my footing. I crashed into the wall of the bathroom which had a metal plate running down its side. My face was gashed badly across the forehead and lay gaping nauseatingly. Sensing I was badly injured, I buzzed for the attendant who took a look at me promptly threw up, then rushed to find the Judge.

When the Judge looked at the cut he panicked then threw up thinking my scull had ruptured and that my brain was oozing out. He thoughtfully threw up again then inquired about any doctors on board the train. Thank God he was the Judge and not the Doc with insight like that, I thought.

Pandemonium ensued as the Judge shrieked that the train be stopped to get me to a hospital when he found there was no medical staff on board the train itself. The attendant in fact found a nurse who assured the Judge what he was seeing was severed muscle tissue, not brain and most importantly she didn't think the cut had fractured the skull nor penetrated the brain.

Unbelievably the Judge's insistence we be let off the train was surprisingly complied with though they said "Sir, we cannot let your friend off the train until we reach a stop where we have a ticket office." The Judge held the bandage tightly against my head to help stop the bleeding. He begged the attendant to continue to seek out any doctor that may be travelling on the train for his friend Doc.

He still demanded we be let off the train at the next stop, which happened to be Jacksonville. Advance arrangements had been made there for an ambulance to be waiting to ferry us to ER of the local hospital. Coincidentally, a few weeks earlier I'd had another incident requiring a visit to the ER when a bathroom towel rack broke off the wall landing on my toe and requiring stitches.

In that ER in Jacksonville the young Japanese doctor asked me, "Why are you here and what can I do for you?" Delirious and obviously in shock I tell him I need stitches removed from my toe. After careful evaluation the young doctor advised, "I suggest that first we put some stitches in here and then take some out there. Does that work for you?" he asked me in a droll no nonsense tone.

The injury required 150 stitches, 75 inside the wound and 75 to close up. The next morning the Judge and I took a flight to Atlanta with me sporting a black eye and patched with an enormous bandage over the right side of my face. We attended the football game the next day where the Judge delighted in telling people that my injury was the result of trying to protect a girl's honor in a bar in Yee Haw Junction, Florida as a dozen rednecks attacked me. The Judge told them I'd held them off single-handedly like a true warrior until one cracked me over the head with a liquor bottle.

It's like Amos and Andy. It all seems silly to everyone else, but not to them. The frat boy side of the two just kept coming out.

Take Your Veggies and Shove Them

The Judge hated to be constrained and lived the authentic embodiment of the "don't fence me in" spirit. He loved meat and potatoes, Wild Turkey, good people of honesty and integrity. He was the original "live and let live" pro-totype. Once in Hollywood while visiting a couple of record companies to promote one of the Judge's bands, we set off in search of a cozy place to eat. It was still early, eleven-ish, so restaurants were still virtually empty.

We found a place that was entirely empty and this was very good as it meant we could freely talk about the previous day's business that rolled on into the previous night's fun which was just concluding with brunch. We planned to wind down over brunch and debrief our outcome expectations from last night's meetings.

The Judge felt sure we had a deal with Warner Brothers where we'd presented his band. Therefore, he felt justified in his exuberance and desire to celebrate the night before. He was so confident in his deal in fact that we celebrated at a bar near the Warner Brothers office, continued celebrating somewhere in south Los Angeles, went on celebrating somewhere else after that and I also remember many joints being passed as we continued to celebrate in the car while a joint made a peace pipe ceremony look arcane as we passed this celebration pipe back and forth many times on the long ride to the hotel.

The party was just ending with us not getting back to our hotel at all. So here we were many hours and sunrise past, midday approaching, at a restaurant too early for lunch in fashionable La La Land where no one apparently is ever hungry before 2:00 in the afternoon.

It's 11 a.m., we're here, we're starving and irritable. This empty restaurant seems perfect to sit, unwind and discuss in detail the band's prospects with the record labels we'd approached. The Judge wanted to solve the riddle of why one of the record execs never sat during the entire meeting; he just paced around the room for two hours occasionally parking his butt on the side of his desk. I said, "That's easy to answer, his jeans were too tight. He couldn't sit down." "Oh yeah," the Judge says, "Fucking Hollywood flash sucks dude, he probably slipped into a robe after we left."

The Judge orders a "burgie" with a "girl" on the side just as the nervous waiter alarmed at having a customer arrive before 2:00 and he's in unchartered territory so he slides over to place menus on our table even though we'd already made our selections. The waiter in wilting voice and nervous disdain said, "we don't serve "burgers," to which the Judge retorts, "you're fucking crazy." I start reading the menu out loud with escalating anxiety about the apoplectic fit I fear the Judge will have at any moment when he finds we've arrived at a tofu bar. The waiter labors with his "special of the day" offerings in case any of these capture the imagination of the now beet red Judge. Vegetarian special of the day, tofu on fresh greens, garnished with more tofu. To add insult to injury the waiter followed this up by asking what the Judge meant by, "a girl on the side?" The eruption was volcanic, immediate and withering.

The Judge went on mumbling something about "a hamburger and a cold beer on the side," as he struggled to maintain his rage he then stood to his full 6' 4" stature staring the waiter squarely down through his one good eye and dazzling eye patch on the other.

As he got out of his chair he stepped ever so slightly away from the table, then reached back with his left hand and flipped the table over, then we turned and walked out. We went back to the hotel and ordered filet mignons. I told the Judge I thought the walk did us both some good. Now, I hoped was a good time to tell him that I didn't think the record deal was going to happen. I sensed the execs were looking for another "Boston" and we were bringing them something from the future. The band was brilliant.

Turn this Fucking Boat Around

Then there was a boat cruise out of the Port of Miami at the special invitation of Seals and Crofts. It was a beautiful 90 footer or thereabouts that appeared to be from the 1940's. The plan included the boat ride out of Miami, two nights at the Coconut Grove Hotel. "Hell yeah!" the Judge said, "Bring on the Diamond Girl duo, dude."

As the boat eased away from the dock I told the Judge that I'd get us some food and a couple of beers. Below deck there was a huge table with an eclectic smorgasbord on display to entice guests on top. I'd already spotted it on my way to the bar to arrange our drinks.

I already had a sinking feeling as I quickly spotted everyone in the mingling crowd was drinking what appeared to be champagne or wine. Oh shit! I asked the bartender if I might have St. Pauli Girl. He answered, "We only have cider or sparkling water. This is a non-alcoholic cruise Sir." Oh My God!

To ease the alcohol bombshell I decided to stop by the smorgasbord on my way back to the Judge to placate him with some delicious carnivorous morsels. Shit, shit, more bad news it was a full vegetarian buffet and the only morsels and hors d'oeuvres to my horror, were mung beans this, tofu that, brussel sprout something else and the guarantee of a loose stool for the duration based on the menu, huh? What the!@#$%^&*?

An indelible memory is seared into the retina and inner ear of every individual present on the evening at the sight and sound of the apoplectic Judge at that moment. And as the boat's proud flag flapped happily in the gentle breeze nearby the Judge now fully doubled over against the railing on the stern like that actor in Titanic but instead of an, "I'm King of the world," this was the Judge, original iconoclast roaring, "Are you people fucking crazy, turn this fucking boat around…….. NOW!"

The Judge threatened to jump overboard and swim back to shore until I reminded him "Dude, your Kools will get wet." We finished the cruise throwing broccoli and carrots to the fish with the Judge belting out rock 'n' roll!!!

Rock The Boat…

Your Private Jet
Is Waiting at the Airport

The hand delivered note said that Doc and the Judge should be at the Ft. Lauderdale Executive Airport at 2 p.m. the next day and to come prepared for a surprise trip away for a couple of days. The PS read, "Don't ask why or where you're going." Was it another special gift from the Jazzman? The Judge did his routine run through the men's department at Saks to pick up appropriately fabulous traveling clothes. I got into the shopping frenzy and in several rash impulsive moments also bought black slacks, a white sweater and black boots. We were ready to head to the surprise party, naturally we felt we were beyond dudes at that moment, we were elevated to certified stud dudes who were chick magnets.

At the airport a man dressed in tuxedo style waiter's garb greeted us formally as we arrived at the airport, walking a step or two ahead to escort us onto the private jet. He turned out to be the plane's Captain. On board we found an embarrassment of tempting goodies including food, alcohol, and two hot female flight attendants. We assumed that we'd be stopping somewhere along the way and pick up other guests otherwise we speculated there'd be no need for two flight attendants just for us. The Judge processed the data and quickly nailed it, "Dude, I think we're going to the islands and these are the hulas."

We took off and quickly corrected east over the ocean then started to slowly turn north and therefore away from the islands. We're now speculating, well could be Atlanta, Chicago, New York even Boston but hell right now who cares, right? "Sit back Doc and enjoy the tantalizing excitements on board," suggested the Judge sagely.

Once the plane had leveled off for the remainder of the flight service overdrive began. I had lobster, the Judge had a steak and both of us had "girls" on the side. In New York, there was a limo waiting that took us to the Algonquin Hotel for a very private cocktail party. There were silver and crystal tinker bells on each table which were used to call for service. I suggested it was a bad call to put bells on the table of a room full of rock 'n' rollers, 99 percent of whom were going deaf and I was right.

Despite repeated attempts to get a group tune going with the bells we all failed miserably. The bells only served as a nuisance to hotel guests and as a reminder to most of them that today's young generation was truly rude, insolent and altogether insufferable. We were proof that this generation was interested only in its own immediate gratification no matter what.

We learned at the hotel that we were in New York to attend the American premier of Genesis live at the Philharmonic. The incredible performance climaxed with a jaw dropping pyrotechnics display on stage. Sadly, this scared the Judge out of his seat and right into my lap. Even more regrettably he whispered sheepishly but no less apologetically over the hubbub, "Dude, I think I crapped in my pants." Circumstances later in the evening proved he had done exactly that.

No matter. We went back to his room where he showered and changed into his still unpacked selections from Saks with swing tags still attached. By the time he was ready however we decided to forego the "meet and greet." It was late and quite honestly we couldn't stop laughing long enough to think about anything else except reliving the last few minutes of the concert and the Judges own memorable climax that evening. It was a terrible thing, all manner of otherwise sensible people going around crapping in their pants if you please, in the day.

This movement encapsulates the crapulous 70's.

A Panty-less Princess in a White Dress

The Coconut Grove Hotel was a favorite of the New York record "guys" (absolutely no record girls then) when they were down in Florida on business trips that seemed to last weeks at a stretch. No matter, there were mirrors on the ceiling and those show ponies from NY loved that. When a record rep we called the Candy Man invited us to a party at the Coconut Grove to introduce and showcase his new band, we thought long and hard for a split second about whether we'd bother to attend. The Judge said, "Shit dude it's the Candy Man," and just as the song liltingly promises he then broke into the song, "Yes the Candy Man can, the candy man can 'cause he mixes it with love and makes the world feel good.'" He offered, "Damn dude, we gotta go," and so we did.

And so our own fairy tale that night begins with the Candy Man gushing like a school girl at length about his new girl whom he was naturally eager to show off. He described his new princess as the most beautiful woman money could buy in Miami. She seemed very young, 17 possibly 18. She was indeed as beautiful as a princess. Having dispensed with the business component of the evening the Candy Man was eager to loosen up, to this end he asked the Judge if he had any "ludes dude?" He went on, "You know to throw back with the next round of drinks."

He whispered excitedly that his princess had never had a lude and she was in the mood tonight. Well, far be it for the Judge to deny a princess, so he offered her two. She rather boldly took both and chased them with a shot of tequila. Shortly thereafter, the amorous couple left the table to dance when I whispered to the Judge "Look, Judge she's not wearing any underwear." He said breathlessly, "Dude where have you been, do try to keep up will you?" "No, she's not wearing underwear nowww, earlier in the evening however, she was," he offered his good eye dancing gaily at the visual. In high dudgeon and with his usual mischief I fancy I even detected a brighter than usual sparkle emanating out of the diamond stud in his eye patch at the titillating idea of a panty-less princess.

We watched as Candy Man and his Princess held each other close and swirled round the dance floor during what seemed to be for them a moving slow dance. Within minutes however, the Candy Man was pushing her away and now cursing loudly in Italian… Huh???

He left her on the dance floor then made a beeline first for the men's bathroom to wash his hands then he hurried back to our table where he threw back another shot of tequila picked up his jacket and hissing his words to us …"she crapped all over herself, look at her."

Tequila, ludes and rock 'n' roll was just too much for his princess. She wanted to let it all hang out and evidently so did her bowel, spontaneously obliging at that very inopportune moment. Crap oozed quickly now staining her diaphanous white dress and so this now humiliated and sullied princess "left the building" with the Judge and the Doc.

Candy Man told us she was ours if we wanted her but we just wanted to get her cleaned up and sent home with a modicum of dignity. We knew no taxi driver would permit her to enter a cab in her present state. So, we quickly left with her, then sobered her up upstairs, and urged her to take a shower. During this time room service had her dress washed out, now we were finally able to put her in her now clean dress and into a waiting taxi. We checked her purse for ID and address and wrote it down for the taxi driver then we sent her off. We never saw this princess again.

The Devil's Triangle

A new guy in town had his pilot's license and asked if we'd like to fly to the Bahamas to gamble. We thought about it long and hard for a split second and said yes. We asked a friend if he'd like to come along. The flight to Freeport in a single engine four seat plane only took 30 minutes or so. Thirty minutes later the Judge had already gone through $1,000 on the craps table was pissed off and ready to return home. We each gave him money to keep him gambling and drinking a few more hours.

The pilot rounded us all up around 2 a.m. and said that he had news of a front moving in. He advised if we didn't beat it we could be socked in for a few days. We were, incidentally, flying visual since the pilot was not instrument rated. By the time we realized the seriousness of the situation and finished checking out of the hotel then getting to the airport it was nearing sunrise. The weather seemed pretty calm and our takeoff was textbook smooth.

A few minutes into the flight the pilot asked if I'd like to fly the plane for awhile. To this end he set the bearings for 270' and suggested I simply hold it steady. Ten minutes into the flight it felt like the plane had hit a brick wall. He took the wheel and dropped below the clouds as the plane began to be tossed around. We'd hit the oncoming front as brutally as if we'd hit a freight train.

The pilot contacted Miami Radar, pushed the "ident" button then gave the tower our approximate location and finally asked to be identified on radar. The Judge was asleep. Miami came back with, "sorry, cannot identify you on radar." We had now been airborne for approximately 25 minutes on what we thought would be another 30 minute flight back to Ft. Lauderdale. We reported our approximate location to Miami as somewhere between Bimini and Ft. Lauderdale, heading due west.

We've now been in the air for over 45 minutes and are flying as low as possible but couldn't stay completely below the clouds and couldn't spot land anywhere. Repeated requests to be identified by Miami Radar were unsuccessful.

An hour into the flight the three of us were by now in a serious panic.

All of us except the Judge who was still snoozing were looking out the window for any sight of land or other aircraft. We were lost in the Devil's Triangle. Ten minutes later, a brief opening in the clouds revealed what we recognized as Key Biscayne below. We had drifted south of Ft. Lauderdale while at the same time making very little forward progress due to the front. Finally, the pilot contacted the tower and reported our location; made a 180° turn, banked left, and flew up the coastline towards Ft. Lauderdale.

We got emergency clearance to land and went in with the very strong cross wind now blowing hard against us. The pilot made a one-point landing and quickly turned to taxi to the gate. This is when The Judge woke up and said to the pilot, "nice landing, dude, let's do it again real soon." A few weeks later the pilot invited our receptionist for a midnight flight over South Florida, whereupon, he put the plane on auto-pilot and forced himself on her. We quickly clipped this randy rooster's wings.

Little red rooster, too lazy to crow by day ... fully 20 years before the Stones.

Tee it High and Let it Fly, Son

The Judge learned many of life's important lessons such as golf, cursing, drinking, and gambling in his formative years as a caddy at a country club in Michigan. The Judge caddied for the pros at the Buick Open, and was a devoted member of Arnie's Army. He was a scratch golfer who was often mistaken on the golf course for Alice Cooper.

Once when the two teed it up, pictures were being taken of each of them, with fans unsure who was the real Alice. The Judge appeared to be the star to the crowd that had gathered around the 18th green as the round was finishing. He looked like a star. He birdied the last hole, picked his burning Kool up off the green then signed a couple of autographs and rushed to the bar. Alice signed autographs until the last person left then joined us.

On another memorable occasion, the Judge asked me to join him for a round at Inverrary Golf club, which was Jackie Gleason's course. Gleason lived across the lake from me and I saw him most mornings driving his Rolls Royce Golf Cart to the clubhouse as I pulled away to the office, but I digress. We were on a par 5 with the Judge pondering what to hit on his second shot, and since he had no depth perception he asked me if I felt he could hit away. Although I'd just taken up golf I knew how to spot the yard markers, to this end I pointed out the 250 yard marker, estimated he was at least 275 yards from the green and factored in a slight wind toward him.

He asked if anyone was on the green. I retorted, "What difference can that possibly make, you can't reach it anyway right?" Famous last words, the Judge connected with a perfect three wood that started low to beat the wind then took off like a pro shot, finally landing near the green, or so we thought. "Damn dude, I killed that son of a bitch, it felt real good Doc," he queried on "Is it OK, did I miss the water?" We got in the golf cart picked up my third shot which I had dribbled 100 yards or so and drove toward the green.

About a hundred yards out I told The Judge that there was a group of five on the green and they were all looking back at us. As we got a little closer I told him that I thought one of the golfers was that fat, angry, asshole Jackie Gleason. "Ah shit, I hit into the fat bastard didn't I," he said with a pirate grin.

As we approached the green we saw Gleason standing staring us down as we approached him to apologize for hitting into them. He's rhythmically tossing the golf ball in question up and down in his right hand. We heard someone in the group say that we'd hit Jackie Gleason in the back with a golf ball. Whoop-ee!

As we walked over the bridge to the green to express how sorry we were, Mr. Gleason brushed past the Judge and said, "Best golf shot I never saw son, don't you ever fucking do that again," his brush-by almost pushed the Judge into the water.

A couple of weeks later as I was leaving for work I noticed Gleason's golf cart was submerged in a canal. Apparently he'd driven off the golf cart path on his way home from the 19th hole the night before. I woke the Judge then drove to his place to pick him up whereupon we grabbed a bottle of black shoe polish and planned some morning mischief. We drove back to Gleason's golf cart and painted a message on the dry side of the cart. It read, "Don't you ever fucking do that again!"

And … away we go!

Woodstock

The Judge admired what Woodstock stood for. He would have liked to have done his own concert of this magnitude and purpose. However, he abhorred the guys in the three-piece suits who always seemed to hijack these things. It became something of a running joke as everyone we met in bars throughout South Florida purported to have attended Woodstock. He'd say "Shit Doc, if all these people attended Woodstock then where were we, did we really miss something here?"

The Judge called the phony Woodstock attendees "Wood Stalkers." So when we came across one he'd announce the "stalker" wanted to buy the bar a round of drinks in the spirit of peace and love. Surprisingly he generally got away with it and many regulars got freebee after freebee this way. We came to the conclusion that vanity was a great instrument for separating a fool and his money.

When Artie Kornfeld, the guiding light behind Woodstock came into our lives we got "lifetime tight." Artie was one of the first free spirits we'd come across. He was a gifted producer and song writer, he was a story teller, hustler, and epitomized the spacey flower power child of that 60's revolution. He had an infectious laugh and always laughed far louder and with greater gusto than his thoughtful and well modulated speech betrayed. "Dusha" is how my wife refers to Artie, which in Slavic refers to a "good and authentic soul."

Artie always had goodies, drank Wild Turkey with us and seemed to always appear with a lovely girl on his arm who hung off his every utterance. Artie never told the Judge he'd discovered that when those "11 shots of Turkey with a girl on the side" were produced in a bar that on my end was invariably lined up 11 shots of tea. No one could keep up with the Judge on this score and I never wanted to try. I was "discovered" by Artie however once when he was impatient to get to the next round and so he reached over, grabbed, then downed one of my shots and balked realizing quickly it was in fact a shot of tea. It became a secret and bond between the two of us. I was the business end of our dynamic duo and there was no way I'd be able to function if I'd stayed toe to toe with the Judge who reigned supreme, and unchallenged, as chief imbiber.

On one memorable occasion the Judge slipped just his head into my office as he leaned into the doorway and teasingly whined like a pouty child in big trouble might do. "Doc, Artie's in the parking lot and won't come out of his car," he then pressed on with gathering concern saying, "Doc, the car doors are locked and it's got to be 100 degrees out there and who knows how much more it is inside the car dude." Years later Artie tried to persuade me with a twinkle the size of Venus in the night sky that the reason he wouldn't get out of the car was because he was on an important call on his cell phone. Liar, liar pants on fire Artie. Duh dude there were no cell phones in 1975…"Oh," he postulated, "I must have been playing with my Rubik's Cube…or something, you know I love that stuff."

Artie is one of my favorite house guests. When he's in town I know I will always see the sunrise and sunset no matter how cold or hot because he insists we always make the time for the deeply spiritual and the boldly spectacular. Then back in the house I hear his sonorous tones erupting from his bedroom like a bunk mate at summer camp, "Doc, you asleep yet?" "No, not yet Artie, but I'm getting sleepy. Are you getting sleepy Artie?" "Yeah, I'm getting sleepy." "Good night Artie." "Good day Doc."

I'll Get You Up in My Pickup

Word reached us that we had been chosen for a special ride in a pickup in Texas. An up and coming songstress was offering moonlight rides in the back of her pickup truck to those who helped break her new song on the radio. "Shit Doc the song is pretty good … and we love Texas, let's do it dude …" drooled the ever ready Judge.

When we finally arrived in Texas we decided to make a detour at Justin Boots before moving on to our date with destiny at the ranch. We each bought a pair of canvas high top zip-up rhinestone boots. The Judge selected light blue boots while I bought green. Finally in equal measure, adding drama and to showcase our love for all things Texan we walked out wearing white 10 gallon Stetson's.

So we finally got to the ranch feeling and hopefully looking like real cowboys. Naturally the question of who goes first was yet to be negotiated. Just as we started a round of rock paper scissors to help determine this protocol we were abruptly stopped with "What's wrong with you boys? Are you bashful or something? Well, there's no need to be, my pickup's bed in the back is cozy for two or three; your choice." It was our amorous songbird abruptly putting an end to our unresolved negotiations with a perky but slutty, "Hop in boys!"

A Texas "bed and breakfast."

The three of us piled into the front seat, she drove us about 30 miles outside Dallas where we parked, hopped into the back of the truck. She then removed the cover off a fresh linen covered mattress apparently custom fit for her truck bed. "Ingenious, yet slutty," the Judge whispered to me. "This dramatically cuts the fixed costs of a thousand and one shaggy nights dude."

What happened? Oh a couple bottles of Southern Comfort, a few joints, guitar playing, a few songs, a few shooting stars, and countless thank-you's delivered full throat and full thrust delivered fast, live and sweaty from our horizontal princess. She was fully engaged and delivered with such command and dexterity we knew this starlet was more Lolita than Lolita. Even our own pushing the boundaries lifestyle seemed a little prim in contrast. We struggled to not betray our shock of the day's and night's offerings.

You could say she was starring in her own down home "meat and greet" in true rock 'n' roll style. We saw the sunrise thru the side and rear mirrors as we drove back to Dallas the next morning. The Judge and I had just experienced our first case of what we came to understand as a variation on plug-ole! Quite unbelievably as we left her she looked back and hissed, "You boys aren't the kiss and tell type are you?" What on earth could she have been afraid of, tongues wagging about her I thought to myself? We offered up perplexed, "No ma'am, our lips are sealed," … in unison as though rehearsed and for at least thirty five years it was thus. This easily covers any statute of limitation.

She drove that pickup complete with that much soiled mattress right up the music charts. A few years ago I bought a refurbished red 1965 Chevy pickup as a monument and reminder of that evening under the Texas skies.

We're standing at the ticket counter for our return flight to Florida when a mother and her young son scuttle by us. The young man says, "Look mamma, look at the cowboys!" I never looked around but heard the mother answer very quickly after it was obvious she had taken a glance at us, "Come along son those aren't cowboys!"

Ooouch! "Should've seen these two cowboys ridin' the range last night bitch," I thought to myself.

Sir, that Ump is Blind

Joe Namath was a partner in a Ft. Lauderdale night club called The Bachelor's Three. They always showcased the top entertainment of the day. The Judge and I and our makeshift team got into a routine of playing softball with the groups who'd performed there. We played spirited games against bands like the Temptations, the Four Tops, Kenny Rogers, and others. In the Kenny Rogers game we played in full elegant tuxedos. A lot of extra sliding into the bases took place for the fun of ripping up the black slacks, dinner coats, and white shirts, who wouldn't? It made you want to play with full grunt, gusto and aggression.

On one such occasion Joe Namath made an appearance at our event to auction a pair of shoes for charity that he'd worn in a big Jet's game. Ray Charles was enlisted to umpire, and he patiently sat behind the fence at home plate in 95 degree Florida heat. He too was elegantly decked out in a full tux. He enigmatically yet earnestly called balls and strikes with a twinkle in his black glasses and great joy in his voice which garnered uproarious glee from delighted spectators.

This game was the highlight of the season and high water mark against which all other games came to be measured. The sublime is no easy measure at all. We loved Ray Charles and he made it clear he liked the dudes right back. Ray sat next to his associate, listening intently as the pitcher delivered the ball to the plate. "Strike one," he shrieked in full throat thrilling the crowds with his unimpeachable umpiring then throwing up his "left" arm to punctuate his calls of conviction. He owned the crowd that day and after a few calls, chanting erupted from the crowd who couldn't believe their luck, it was priceless they joyously, respectfully, adoringly cried, "You're blind ump," throughout the entire game.

The cheering and jeering delivered that day came with jubilation, love and reverence for the master and his ability to laugh with them. It was magical. Ray called every pitch for the entire game, he held firm on calls, he even dusted home plate a couple of times. The final tour de force came when he threw a player out of the game for arguing one of his calls. The game had the flavor of a real hometown ball game. I know Ray enjoyed himself because he talked about it during his performance that night.

"Tell me ... What'd I say?"

Keith Moon is Dead

It's a couple of hours after the Who's concert and we're back at the hotel after the incredible show in Miami's Baseball Stadium. Keith Moon stepped into our elevator, which coincidentally or perhaps not was packed with lots and lots of fucked up people. He was wearing a tuxedo and seemed oblivious to everything but that the elevator was indeed going "down" as he needed.

Coincidentally, even I remember this one as if through a deep haze. Keith leaned against the back wall of the crowded elevator seeming to be in some deep trance. He continued gently, sensually rubbing his shoulders back and forth along the back wall as if moved by a higher power, swaying to some hypnotic rhythm heard only by him. He didn't speak, he didn't notice anyone in the elevator, just went on swaying and sliding in a euphoric reverie reminiscent of the famous Whirling Dervish. Only he was privy to the sense and purpose of this imperative.

Not long afterwards we learned Keith Moon had overdosed on medication he was reportedly taking to wean him off alcohol. Ironically he died in the same room Cass Elliot of The Mammas and the Pappas had died in four years earlier.

Keith Moon was dead, holy cow dude, what the @#%&()(*^%#@!? I hope he exited in peace but I feel sure he left us silently swaying to that imperative described above. Police reports indicate there were 32 pills in his stomach with 26 of these not yet digested or dissolved by his system.

Yes, I Can See For Miles And Miles…..

Charlie Daniels

"Book me two seats Doc. Hell you know the routine, one for me and one for my fiddle," he'd say quietly when we asked him to commit to worthy charity events we might count on him to lend his name and contribute his talent toward. He's known around the world for his generosity and incredible charitable work, Charlie is always looking for and finding ways to give back. This is a story about Charlie Daniels, one of America's and country music's own living national treasures.

Our experience with Charlie started right at the beginning of the rock side of his career, as his star took off on its meteoric rise. He's still doing it all today with his zeal for his craft, for his loyal followers who adore him, his voice and what he stands for. The Judge and I called them "Charlie's Zealots."

SHE was the first major city rock station to play *Uneasy Rider*. We dubbed the song onto cassette from the album and listened to it about 50 times while driving up and down I-95 late into the night. "Shit, this is good. Let's go back to the station and see what it sounds like on the air," the Judge said. He knew there was a place for this song on this rock station. I don't think anyone could deny that Charlie Daniels has given more back to his fans, charities, and to our troops around the world than any other artist. If he knew you needed him he'd be there.

He was with us again in Ft. Lauderdale supporting severely handicapped children, however this time Charlie was also to be awarded a "key to the city." When we walked into the children's center it sadly appeared they seldom had seen people from outside the institution, perhaps only an occasional family visitor. They rushed towards us pulling at our clothes, arms, some sat on the floor and tugged at our pants. They were so excited it appeared each of them was coping with their swirling emotions in their own way.

One young girl who appeared to be about thirteen jumped into Charlie's arms wrapping her arms and her legs around him. In her excitement she peed all over him. He hugged her back then graciously proceeded to the podium for the presentation so moved by these children's needs and plight to care about the warm urine all over his clothes. I saw what had happened, I also saw the urine dripping down his pants to the floor as she hugged him and then on stage when he gave his acceptance speech.

I remember one time Charlie turning to me and saying as we walked onto the green at the #2 hole at the Gainesville Country Club "I have a feeling Doc, an idea that country rock's going to be huge on FM." The idea was formulating in his mind and he urged on "We ought to buy up all em' FM suckers and launch the format in Jacksonville, Florida home of Lynard Skynard." Yes Charlie. Damn, we should have!

Doc and Charlie Daniels circa 1983

Growing Pains

The Judge was quick to bore, period. If he felt things weren't as he felt they ought to be, or if he couldn't get Jazzman's support on an issue, he'd first pout petulantly, then he'd vanish.

Once driving home, listening in the car to the Judge on the radio, I heard the repetitive scratch, scratch of the needle hitting the turntable's capstan. My first thought was the Judge's gone to the bathroom and the record had run out. For no reason at all I turned to look at traffic about me waiting at a stop sign and quite unbelievably there he was, the Judge in his Judge GTO right beside me!

Judge the car, and in it Judge the Dude looking sheepish. My first thought was shit, it's the Judge, what the @#$%&*)(*&^%#@! We locked eyes for a nanosecond, then the Judge tore off in "his Judge" leaving a dust cloud behind him and about me. I valiantly chased him for about a quarter mile then finally realized I was needed more urgently at the station, so I reluctantly determined I'd rush back to man the controls for the remainder of his shift.

The Judge had walked out mid tune and was urgently heading to the airport. He called me a couple days later. "Dude, it's me, I'm in La La Land." He confided he'd finally realized he's "dyslexic" which he felt mitigated his failure to focus. He followed on passionately with "Dude, the pressure's just too much. OK?" "I just needed to get away for awhile."

I never fully understood how being dyslexic would affect a strapping 6' 4" adult male with only one good eye and a leather eye patch on the other and he for his part never attempted to explain it. Ah, the sweet mystery of life…

Ladies and gentlemen lo and behold the Judge is finally growing up and beginning to experience pressure.

The Playbook

The Judge, the Jazzman and I played poker a couple times a month in the off-season with a Dolphins football player with whom we did business, the great all pro left guard, Bob Kuchenberg. The Judge lived and breathed Dolphins, Gators and Wolverines but particularly the Dolphins after their perfect season in 1972. For this particular preseason game between Miami and the Rams both the Judge and I decided to overnight it in a hotel and take a taxi to the game.

We were on our way having just left a relaxing session at the hotel bar; we then planned to make a pit stop as we left the hotel. I was still indisposed when I heard the Judge squeal excitedly, "Doc, Doc there's a Rams' playbook over here. What do you think, can I have it?" Doc's approval gave the Judge ownership of what then was considered the Bible for a professional football player, particularly a rookie.

We adjusted our plans and quickly detoured back to our room to look over the playbook. We spotted the name Steve Jones stenciled across it. On our way back down the elevator to head to the game we had the pleasure of landing with Cal Rosenbloom, the owner of the Rams. The Judge opened his jacket a stitch revealing the book then whispered, "Boy do we have a surprise for you." In fact we didn't learn much from the playbook except for their assertion of a perceived weakness in the Dolphins game and the first offensive play they planned to run.

I convinced the Judge we ought to try to get the playbook back to the player who was probably in big trouble. To this end, we headed back to the lobby, nothing but "Rams" on our minds. The Judge bravely and rather boldly boarded the team bus which was cranked, humming and ready to go. He cheekily borrowed the driver's microphone and announced in a sissy, girly voice adding a hissy lisp, "Oh Steve, Steve Jones? I have something for you, meet me in room 427 you naughty boy."

We both turned round then bolted toward the elevator running into the first one that sprang open, banged on the up button until it obliged. Within seconds of us entering and securely locking the door we hear the unmistakable thud on the room's door.

The Judge jumped to action standing in the middle of the room coquettishly holding the playbook as I began to open the door. I inched the door ajar and the rookie rushed in grabbed the book then with all his might pushed the Judge against the wall. This rookie's memories of his first trip to the Orange Bowl must surely include running wildly down the hall, now reunited with his playbook, toward the bus.

Behind him the prankish jeers of the Judge shrieking for a little respect taunting, "What, not even a thank you?" He paused for effect, "You ungrateful, inconsiderate, son-of-a-bitch, may your ear holes turn into ass holes and crap all over your no good shoulders you ungrateful cretin," and ending with a memorable "Go Dolphins"…

This is Howard "I'm Just Telling it Like it Is" Cosell

The Judge and I are in New York for a meeting with ABC. In time the meeting winds down and soon we're heading down in an elevator back to the lobby and out into the intoxication of sights, sounds and smells that is Manhattan. Before we get to the lobby however the elevator stops and the doors open and we're brought back to earth with the irritation of our sudden and unwelcome delay. Well, before the Judge got a chance to vent his annoyance in crisp colorful expletives he looked up gasping as the great one, Mr. Cosell, walked in smoking his signature industrial grade and size cigar.

The elevator is quickly infused with the aromatic smoke and we watch it dance and lilt throughout every corner of the small space. The Judge shoots me a look then whispers "Damn bro, that thing would last me all day. Watch this 'rope a dope.'" I now know exactly where he's heading with his thought then caution him, "Careful Judge, he's straight and an attorney of some repute." I then turned to the source of the smoke, by now the elevator could be mistaken for a Swedish steam bath.

"Mr. Cosell," the Judge presses on, anxious not to miss an opportunity like a child who crams with Santa regarding every possible toy wish while he has Santa's full attention in his lap. "Mr. Cosell …" he goes on bravely, "I've never seen a cigar as grand as that one. Hell, its enormous dude." The Judge was buttering up Mr. Cosell. Cosell knew it and I suspect loved it. Sensing the benign tone of Cosell's response the Judge ventured forth boldly, "I have a proposition for you," as he reaches into his jacket pocket and pulls out a joint in short order.

"I'll trade you this for that cigar, its great shit dude, homegrown … rabbit tobacco!" Enjoying the drama Cosell chuckles then without missing a beat says "Sure kid, you got yourself a deal, enjoy." "Oh you too, Mr. Cosell," the Judge winks back. I don't know what Howie, as the Judge called him, did with the loco weed.

Once the elevator arrived then opened in the lobby all three of us again become visible as the thick smoke dissipated, it was a quintessential cartoon moment. My memory remains vivid of the Judge taking a toke on the cigar then minutes later ditching it on the sidewalk. "Damn dude," he hissed, "this shit's terrible." Proof again, friends that packaging and size doesn't equal satisfaction.

I can't get no satisfaction dudes ... no, no, I can't get me no ... !

You Boys Know Neil Young?

Our homage to Woodstock was getting underway on a newly dedicated 50 acre park in downtown Miami. It was to be free to all citizens and music lovers, corporate sponsors would see the value of a prominent position for their product and their money helped offset the massive cost of this ambitious undertaking. We felt confident we'd attract over a 100,000 people.

The bands donated their time and absorbed personal costs thereby fully donating their resources in the charitable spirit of the event. The Judge held a conviction that this epic concert was to be done "right." This meant only professionals were to be hired for everything pertaining to management of the event, however promotion remained the responsibility of Doc and the Judge. We didn't trust anybody would dedicate adequate time and energy needed to get as near to perfect as humanly possible.

To this end, we were busy yet again pouring over the schematic of the concert layout in my office when the Jazzman came in, all 300 pounds of him and joyfully announced someone named Neil Young called asking to participate in the show, further he'd be here in about 30 minutes to discuss details.

The Jazzman (God love him) pressed on in middle-aged obliviousness …"Hey, you boys know who this Neil Young is?" "Doc, can we use him?" The Judge and I scoped the window and eventually a 1955/6 Ford station wagon drove into the parking lot. Neil got out of the car on the passenger side and came into the building.

He said he'd been listening to SHE on his boat in Ft. Lauderdale. He said he'd heard about the event and wanted to know if we had room for him. He shyly added the date of the event was in fact his birthday and he'd wanted to participate if there was room for him as it was a great cause.

The Judge and I thought long and hard about his offer for a split second then eagerly agreed; we then asked if he'd go on air that very moment and announce his participation in the show which was now only 7 weeks away. He was happy to and with business concluded we said grateful good-byes in the parking lot. We sent him away with a cassette recording of the interview he'd just announced.

As word spread about Neil Young's involvement and with phones ringing off the hook, we nervously begin rethinking plans to accommodate more than 250,000 spectators. We had no further contact with Neil as there was no specific need to do so. However, shortly thereafter his manager called, "What the hell's this concert Neil's committed himself and the band to?" He added for good measure, "And who the hell's going to pay for his appearance?"

Apparently Neil casually dropped the cassette off on his manager's desk asking him to listen to it. Thinking it was a tape of a new song it wasn't listened to immediately. I placated this zealot calmly explaining it was a charity event and that all the musicians were donating their time and expenses. To take a chess analogy to its full conclusion he "saw" my facts and raised a check mate by screaming the longest tirade of expletives my not so virgin ears had ever endured. Then with a clank the line was dead, he'd hung up.

Neil Young appeared on stage with a 35-piece, chart reading, orchestra, most of them wearing earmuffs to soften the volume of the loud rock 'n' roll. Who paid the freight? Just as he said he would, Neil Young faithful to his word, paid for everything as did every act appearing that night.

The star studded event was emceed by the two headliners from Doctor Hook, Dennis and Ray. The Miami police were keeping a lookout with infrared cameras from the top of the Miami Herald Newspaper building to spot any use of illicit drugs or alcohol. As evening approached and with anticipation for Neil Young's appearance looming large with the audience, the crowd swelled to well over the estimated 250,000 people.

Night fell in magnificence as beautifully as in a fairy tale and for the pleasure of the gathered crowd Dr. Hook's Full Medicine Show was getting ready to take the stage, just then we lost power over the entire neighborhood. The only light visible was flashlight, the sporadic light coming from vendors and by first aid stations and the like who had generators. We felt palpable emotion gathering from the mammoth crowd like a tightly coiled snake ready to unleash.

Clearly we knew over 250,000 of them were there but with the blackout they were invisible except for the electric force of their collective energy. Nonetheless we couldn't see them and worse we couldn't communicate with them. Suddenly we saw the flicker of a cigarette lighter glow warmly here and there. Before long every individual in that audience seemed to catch this zeitgeist and all at once it seemed that 250,000 cigarette lighters were emblazoned in perfect synchronicity and the ambience at that moment was magical.

Needless to say the police were particularly curious about why the people needed lighters unless of course they intend to light those crazy and illicit joints as soon as the podium dims down for that no good and corrupting rock music. Still as those thousands of cigarette lighters kept vigil providing a hypnotic, hazy canopy of light over the crowd songs suddenly spontaneously swirled from the crowd and under the cover of darkness people sang, hummed and performed their own a cappella versions of their favorite pop songs.

In the darkness, the crowd eagerly jockeyed for prime positions edging their way to find a spot of ground closer to the stage. We sensed their forward movement but had absolutely no way to communicate to stop them. By now the crowd crush had pushed people in the front to breaking point with the magic beginning to turn to frustration. Now some of the wooden barricades skirting the front of the stage began to crack and a young pregnant girl was literally forced sideways thru an opening ending up on the ground under the stage. Paramedics worked with her by flashlight until the ambulance arrived. I think she gave birth to a baby girl. Our own Woodstock was kicking into high gear.

About thirty minutes into the blackout, I was told that Dennis and Ray wanted to see me in their motor home. They were eager to share an idea with me about how to get control of the crowd back as soon as the power came back on. If you know anything about these great guys you know it probably wasn't an old fashioned sing-a-long. I'd known the boys for a while and I was sure as I was standing there that there'd be nothing quaint about anything they'd sing.

Still, Ray urged, "Doc I know you're under a lot of pressure right now, but this will pass. The power will be restored and things will be fine." He said he had the perfect song to ease the tension when the show resumed. The caveat was … "but, knowing that city officials, police, reporters, others are watching, we wouldn't do the song without your explicit approval, OK?"

Standing nose to nose in the front room of their motor home Dennis and Ray started their own a cappella rendition of, "What you do when you can't get no pussy." "Get it Doc," they asked like naughty schoolboys then continuing, "after a few verses everyone will join in and the tension will disappear, what do you say Doc?" I told them that I didn't see a problem with them reopening the show with the song but I wanted to check with a couple of people first. I told them that I would be at the top of the steps as they came onto stage and based on the final decision I'd signal a final OK or not to them by a thumbs up, or thumbs down as conversation would be impossible over the applause. They agreed to go along with my wishes. Naturally the Judge and I gave it earnest consideration for a split second and gave it two gigantic thumbs up!

Dennis, Ray, and the Medicine Show were ready to go on stage as soon as power was restored. I positioned myself at the top of the steps so they'd catch my hand signal as they went on stage. As luck would have it the person leading them on stage by flashlight stumbled and fell into me thereby knocking me over. As I hurtled toward the floor I was unable to signal the boys eagerly awaiting the anticipated thumbs up sign …

As Dennis and Ray missed seeing my 'thumbs up' they remained true to their word and didn't do the song. Two weeks later I received an unmarked cassette in the mail with a hand written note attached reading, "Where were you Doc, you were supposed to give us a signal to do the song, dude?" On the cassette were Dennis and Ray giving me a hard time about being a prude followed by yet another a cappella of "What you do when you can't get no pussy."

From that moment one of my abiding goals became to bring my career full circle and return to doing what I loved so much in the beginning … being an authentic DJ, although it may be decades down the road. Authenticity is tragically under-rated in our poll and rating driven chaotic lives. I admire it, I see it seldom, it's unmistakable when found in an individual and remains for me the mark of an individual living with authorship over his or her life. Authenticity is the capacity to live every moment and draw every breath with exacting exaltation from moment by moment.

When authenticity has a currency again and I hope this day comes sooner rather than not I know this original recording by those wonderful wizards from Dr. Hook and their dazzling song will surely be heard again.

Backstage was always a rollicking experience.
Can you spot a young Nicolette Larson in the pic? Doc is fourth from the left, top row.

Thanks from the Doobie Brothers.

Listen up, and keep your ears peeled for the naughty bits! Amongst the collection is a tape of Howard Stern live on WWWW-FM (W4) in Detroit. God, he was great even back then. And other goodies … the Judge and I were notorious for carrying a concealed cassette recorder into parties!

ZZ Top

And the motorcade rolls on!

The Judge and I liked the annual trip to Dallas and Ft. Worth for ZZ Top's New Year's Eve Show. We have a convoy of limos so long going to the gig that I'm secretly convinced lined up all those limos might have covered the width of Texas.

In truth the limos from Dallas to Ft. Worth numbered over 40. But, you don't go to Texas without a stop at an authentic Tex Mex roadhouse, naturally on this occasion too it was a must for the Judge.

A memorable photograph marking this stop one year is the one that appears on this book's cover. There's a rather lovely girl to the Judge's left who was lured into the photo as pictorial proof of the Judge's magnetism over the opposite sex. Truth be told however, he simply told her he'd like her to sit next to him to fully complement and enhance his sense of fabulousness for the photo.

The Judge always liked a pretty girl on his arm even if he'd never seen her before, nor would he ever see her again. It was an even more perfect transaction than prostitution and to top it off an excellent legacy of photos with myriad hot babes whose names he never had to trouble himself to learn.

The girl on my right was mysterious. She laughed with or without company.

Frosty the Snowman

On one particular outing I wore a sumptuous cashmere A&M records sweater that was given to me by an executive at A&M Records. The sweater had an A&M patch sewn onto it representing the A&M Records logo. I wore it as the Judge and I prepared to go to the Cotton Bowl to see Tony Dorsette in his final college game. I was mercilessly jeered at and called a "narc" by Longhorns who saw me as an enemy infiltrator wearing what they saw as a Texas A&M sweater to the game.

On this outing we extended our trip to attend the Dallas/Minnesota playoff game. The Vikings had wanted to spray fake snow onto their sidelines in honor of their routinely snow stacked sidelines back home. Their request was given consideration then denied for whatever reason but there was some residual resentment among their fans throughout the day.

It was obvious that the players wouldn't be able to thrill their supporters with their infamous and much loved slides on the snow. We learned to expect the unexpected however, even we were alarmed to spot a lone fan dressed in full snowman's outfit boldly walking down the aisle towards the Cowboy's bench.

By the time he got to our row he was on fire with flames lapping dangerously, now consuming him from head to toe. His outfit had caught fire from a liquid hand warmer he'd inadvertently brushed against on this walk which apparently belonged to an overzealous Cowboy fan in an aisle seat.

Suddenly, incredibly this flaming snowman is working his way down our aisle with a national live TV feed following his every move. The Judge promptly pooped his pants, "Oops Doc, I did it again," he winced thirty years before Britney Spears. It's fair to say our hero suffered the proverbial loose stool 'tis true.

The Judge then jumped over the seat in front of us. Just as the snowman reached us he was jumped on then beaten down by Dallas fans in an apparent effort to extinguish the flames. Yeah right, wink.

The Judge and I covered our faces from the cameras ashamed to have allowed the snowman to burn and get beaten up to boot. We left immediately high tailing it back to our hotel to drown our shame at the bar. All in all we were very happy to see the final half of the game back here comfortable and in blissful anonymity.

And the Winner Is...

The head of a major record label flew into Ft. Lauderdale to judge a battle of the bands competition the Judge and I were running. His company provided the cash prize so we asked him to officiate, choose the prize winning act and present them with the grand prize.

He came out happy to do the honors, clearly delighted to see us again and thrilled with the chance to squeeze in some fun and sun in Ft. Lauderdale. The winner was set to receive cash, a recording contract and a trip to LA for a recording session.

No doubt foolhardy after the fact, but on the day in question we did give in to the Judge's demands to oversee refreshments and catering. After now clinching the responsibility for catering and refreshments, the Judge decided it didn't actually present the chance for fun or high jinx he'd hoped for. As the time drew near he whispered that the menu for the gala was five buckets of KFC and two garbage bins full of "Purple Jesus."

Purple Jesus is a lethal concoction of pure grain alcohol, mixed with grape juice and other fruits added for flavor as well as to take the edge off. From our own experience, excess consumption combined with a few tokes generally resulted in a whopper of a trip. We called it "trip juice."

Not to be outdone, this exec wanted his share and set to work on memory-making in Ft. Lauderdale, and so he did, though not in the way he'd imagined. By the end of the day, his choice for Florida's best rock band of the year, through his psychedelic purple prism, was a country banjo-picking group.

Hooray, a win for the best band. Certainly not the best band for our market though. In his purple purity he judged truly on talent without consideration for the appropriate pop genre. However heads did roll when he got back to LA when he was asked to report on the curiosity of a country string pickin' band winning the hard rock category on his watch. "Dude, another nasty mother."

As he slipped into his limo for the airport he was handed another glass of Purple Jesus and two joints "to go." Reports reached us thick and fast of him in first class enduring a paranoid, white knuckle ride in the plane. The stewardesses described his demeanor as nonresponsive.

Back in LA and now of clear head he called us asking for a re-count of the vote since his company had no interest in banjo pickers. We soothingly assured him that the best band had indeed been chosen. The lesson for today children: all business decisions should and must be made with a clear mind, or else prepare for the circumstances. Class dismissed.

"Flatt and Scruggs reign supreme!"

A Drink in the Face

Whenever we had business that bought us to LA the Judge and I stayed at the Hotel California, immortalized by the Eagles. On one such visit the Judge was on a collision course with a legendary movie ego in the infamous Polo Lounge. This venue was always swarming with starlets, actors, entertainers and the Judge loved it. The clientele seemed to encompass both many who'd already made it to the top as well as the many others who hoped to be discovered here.

On the night in question however I ended up between this major movie actor, then married to an iconic singer, and his sports nemesis on this night the Judge. They were engaged in a tense no holds barred exchange concerning the merits or otherwise of both the 76'ers and the Lakers. An hour later this conversation had taken a decidedly caustic tone having moved on from sports to outright hostility and personal attacks. Just as the star prepared to hurl his drink in the Judge's face and still unaware of the turn of events, I'd leaned forward to ask the bartender for the check.

The petulant and pouting star was bristling over this brash whipper snapper's insolence and irritating cockiness with the final blow being his impassioned support of entirely the wrong team. He snapped and leaned forward hurling his aperitif in the moment I'd bent down toward the Judge to whisper my plan to head upstairs.

The spirit is airborne and now I'm soaking in the offended star's alcohol. The Judge hisses, "I don't like this son of a bitch Doc, I'll be coming up right behind you dude." We had several more days scheduled in LA and had a late start the next morning. Curiously we awoke to find our hotel accommodations and all bar charges mysteriously taken care of.

Hmmm ... revelation, behold a thespian with a conscience, even the Judge commented, "Turns out that sucker wasn't as bad as all that Doc." In my experience many actors have grown fat and lazy expecting the world to fawn over their every utterance, they expect the heaven and earth to bend to accommodate their every vapid whimsy. He on the other hand turned out to be a very nice man. Doc and the Judge approved of this dudes "mega dudeness." Oh what a world we live in, no wonder it's referred to as La La Land.

Babette is Dead

On another business trip to LA and yet another memorable stay at the Hotel California I'd received an unexpected and upsetting phone call from home. The Judge and a record exec were out and just coming into my room as I'm emerging from the bedroom screaming, "Oh my God Babette is dead, I just can't believe she's dead." In an obvious sign of the decadent times they both assume under the circumstances that Babette's probably a hooker I've had in my room while they were out and that she's probably overdosed and now panicking about the implications of a dead body being discovered in my room.

They're now running wild with consolation and similar personal episodes and I simply couldn't shut them up long enough to explain that Babette was in fact my fifteen-year-old poodle who had deteriorating health lately and had just died. After the ordeal was over and sorted out, after they discovered there was no overdosed hooker nor a body to dispose of, both the Judge and the record executive danced wild eyed and in grand exaltation to the tune of, "What do we do now ho, ho, he, he."

One catastrophic moment quickly spawned another as in this exuberant state the stoned executive stumbled back too close to the fireplace setting his glorious "man mane" and his rather fabulous evening jacket off in flames. Now we have a real emergency. Somebody get this chump a doctor, and possibly an emergency hair transplant.

What a to do…

I set to ripping the jacket off his back, throwing it into the shower while he was taking off his white starched shirt so the Judge could corroborate that he in fact was not on fire himself. On this night I receive the next of many refreshing though unwelcome and unexpected alcohol showers. This time its champagne ordered to celebrate the narrow escape when they realized Babette was my beloved now departed poodle. We make a toast to Babette wishing her many happy years in her new puppy home in the sky.

I don't want a new puppy. I want Babette.

Play it Again Sam...

On this same trip we have a business meeting scheduled with a very senior exec in his office which was decorated to evoke the steamy, sultry decadence inspired I'm sure by a trip to Casablanca or some such exotic locale. The executive was dressed beautifully, coolly but no less elegantly in white silk trousers, crème shirt, and ivory moccasins.

The only movement in the room was the monotonous decadent stirring of the wide blade rattan fan circling lazily like some whirling dervish above our heads in his dimly lit office. Yes, I thought to myself catching a wafting swoosh of warm wind from the rotating vortex above our heads it was indeed ambient.

I imagined it helping to have such a tranquil setting for an office with all the mayhem that's notoriously part and parcel of the record business. Now, we're on our second round of rum shots, his private line starts ringing wildly abruptly bringing us all out of our reverie back into the present.

He shot a look at the phone, gets a tip off from his secretary about the caller and the nature of the call and he says, "Guys, you gotta hear this OK," and as he said that he put the call on the speaker phone. I knew who this was, it was his label's disco superstar who was waking up without. Her desperate, hysterical pleas ended abruptly when he finally relented, then promised to have a package delivered to her home.

She thanked him again and again and promptly offered to pay him for his generosity with her entire share of her brand new album's revenue to guarantee a continuous supply. She let him know she needed to ensure supply going forward whatever the cost.

Another Disco Duck!

Accessory to Arms Smuggling?
No Sir, not this Marine!

I'm working very late one evening and hear someone pounding on the front door. The station is all but empty now save cleaning crew and on air talent. I look out the window and see a young blonde girl and her red custom sports car in the parking lot. I open the door to find a beautiful, elegant woman speaking broken English with a broad French accent; she wants to know which person is responsible for this radio station.

I offered to take full responsibility for whatever message she was there to deliver. She said that she had recently arrived in America and was intrigued by what she heard on the radio station. After a brief conversation she asked that I finish up and go out with her for drinks and dinner, huh? OK.

We're headed north on US 1 out of Ft. Lauderdale when her fancy sports car broke down. She asked me to wait in the car while she made a phone call. Less than an hour later a non-descript, black car arrived followed by a tow truck. In quick time we were headed in the car to her chosen destination, which was a very large, old mansion on Palm Beach. When we entered the house I saw a man sitting by the fireplace with a blanket draped over his knees with a sinister looking associate on guard right behind him. Was I in the presence of the infamous mysterious Saudi arms dealer and billionaire Adnan Khashoggi? She later confirmed that I was.

He hissed, "I told you never to bring strangers into this house. Get him out of here." I consider myself sharp and quickly got the impression I was unwelcome so I carefully backed out of the house, waiting outside for the next move. She came out with car keys in hand and we left shortly thereafter in a BMW ending up at the Breakers Hotel. I heard the surf but rarely saw the ocean for quite a few days.

On the final night, I was told a car would be waiting for me in front of the hotel at 8 a.m. the next morning to take me back to Ft. Lauderdale. "Thank you very much mister and thank you again. Your friend, she would be in touch.

Thank you." Hmmm I thought to myself OK now, isn't this unusual?

I received a postcard a few days later saying that she was returning to the South of France to be with her father who was undergoing brain surgery. She thanked me again for a wonderful time and said she'd be in touch.

Next, two men in black suits arrived at my office with questions about my relationship with the young French lady. Who, what, where, when, why was the basic line of interrogation from the two who introduced themselves to me as government agents. I told them the same story I've shared with you and never heard from them again.

Many months later I received an unexpected parcel that contained a Dallas newspaper. On the cover was a very prominent photograph of this lovely French girl who had been arrested for her part in an arms smuggling deal. She'd been deported and was sending me the article to explain where she was and why there had been no contact throughout the intervening months as she'd promised. Again, she said she'd be in touch when things settled down. She's still an international woman of mystery who I refer to as my "Pussy Galore," just another memorable experience from the 70's.

Snatch 'N' Roll sugar!

What's Good for the Goose...

The Judge and I both sincerely appreciated people in genuine distress. To this end we received an unexpected call from a friend in Chicago saying he wouldn't take no for an answer and planned to be on the next flight to Ft. Lauderdale eagerly wanting to meet us at the famous Polynesian bar, Mai Kai.

Well, imagine our surprise in hearing this knowing as we did his history of severe alcohol dependency and his many successful and difficult years of hard won abstinence. We knew this phone call was a bad sign, we calculated he'd been sober for 25 long years, and even today described himself as a recovering alcoholic.

We knew the call boded badly for him and we immediately recognized the need to help in whatever capacity we could after this disturbing call. The Judge favored a potent drink called Last Rites for desperate situations. This infamous concoction contained 5 rums. Indeed the description on the drinks menu suggested ominously, "Get your affairs in order before this one."

Our friend insisted on trying the famous drink at the Polynesian Room as soon as he arrived, then four rounds of last rites later he found the voice and confidence to share with us that back home he'd unexpectedly returned a day early from a convention he'd attended in Las Vegas. As you might imagine he was astounded to find his wife of many years in bed with the next door neighbor's wife.

What can you offer under the circumstances, and all we could offer after the disclosure, "Dude, everyone says she never deserved you." He seemed to take comfort in the words. We continued on helpfully taking our cues from his reactions and added, "Hey, what's the big deal anyway?"

We suggested he might return home and if the situation was one he could live with as he seemed reluctant to cut off all ties with his wife, "Hell dude, go home and be with your wife - and your new sister-in-law." He seemed to genuinely take solace in our heartfelt advice about it not really being, "You know dude - a biggie."

Who loves you babe? Remind me to tell you the full story sometime about the time we gambled all night with Telly Savalas then suddenly realizing that we were down to $5.00 which didn't cover the cab fare back to the Vegas airport. It was time to roll the lucky number "27."

More Last Rites

We tried to keep yet another friend away from the Polynesian bar and especially away from its "last rites" which he loved way too much, and which we knew drew him in like iron filings to a big magnet. Consequently we always walked a tightrope between being available to get out and about with him if he needed us and the corresponding full time job of keeping him out of trouble.

He had an inexplicable penchant for somehow morphing from perfect American / English into perfect German seamlessly after 2 Last Rites. We quizzed him about this and he'd say, "Guys stop pulling my leg will you." He urged on "Honestly, to my knowledge there's no German ancestry, nor do I have any knowledge of the German language – stop mucking around with me," so this talent remained a mystery to him and us.

On one occasion when he wanted to do it all again we asked German speaking friends to join us (and they spoke impeccable German). After listening carefully they confirmed with disbelief this still inexplicable competency. As usual, the following day our friend had no recollection of his latest Teutonic foray. I think it was easier for him to believe we'd willfully taunt him with lies about such competencies than entertain the netherworld notion that he may indeed inexplicably speaks perfect German.

Well on another occasion not long thereafter, we left the bar shortly after our friend only to find him at a full stop at a green traffic light in his spectacular convertible. He was a vision with his top peeled back sitting in a rising pool of water in the middle of a typical Florida deluge with a blank look on his face shrieking in full throat, not unlike Adolph Hitler in full flight, in German at an officer who'd stopped to check on him.

As expected our friend enthusiastically continued cursing in German, by now in full voice, attracting quite a crowd of onlookers and several more police as well. The Judge was sad for our dear friend and the commotion he'd brought upon himself. He helpfully slipped alongside the senior policemen and told him he was a friend of this man's and that although he couldn't explain his tirade he made a promise to take him right home if they'd allow him to be released into his care.

The Judge finally settled him into the back of "the Judge" then drove back to his own home to sober him up in the Judge's guest bedroom where he could watch over his friend. There was only one remaining issue and with a "shut them damned curtains - dude" order he rolled over and slept for over 24 hours straight. No good deed goes unpunished as we all know.

On a cheerful note however and with all natural light now totally blocked out for several days, he emerged as the chrysalis revived and ready to speak in tongues another day.

The world turns on bad instinct acted upon that turns quickly into very bad decisions, taken in hindsight with the acrimonious and mandatory promises hissed to friends about making better choices next time.

Go on dude do it again.

Dude, Wanna Shoot Some Hoops?

The phone rings and I rush to grab it however my wife gets there first, all I hear on my end is "Well hello there, how have you been?" She goes on … "Aha, aha, aha … sure, fine, fine. OK then let me grab him for you!" She calls out to me letting me know, "It's the Judge, he's wondering if you'd like to go out to shoot some hoops?" Huh???

Well I'm thinking this is a great big departure from our usual routine however perhaps sweating it up on a court and shooting hoops for a few hours may help me work through a particular work predicament I was still resolving to my satisfaction in my mind. "Sure dude, OK I'll get ready and pick you up in 45 minutes." I hang up the phone clear and confident in our plan. I showered, got into shorts, T-shirt and sneakers. I wanted to be sure of the pressure on the basketball, then deciding it needed a little air I pumped it up just a tweak for good measure. Now with all systems go and an unexpected, though increasing welcome, opportunity to burn some aggression on the court I'm in the car on my way to pick up the Judge to shoot some hoops.

I slid into the parking lot at his apartment. I rang the door bell, then he emerged resplendent in exquisite Saturday Night Fever fineries including but not restricted to white polyester pant suit, a shimmering exotically hand painted "open down to there" silk disco shirt and ivory crocodile loafers to complete the magnificence. At that moment he was Tony Monaro before John Travolta ever was. I believe I even glimpsed a medallion bouncing on his hairless chest.

I however am now thoroughly confused. Apparently and for the moment inexplicably so is he. He saw me and he hissed, "Where the fuck are you going in shorts dude?" To which all I could offer was, "Judge, I thought we were shooting some hoops?" He offered a hissed, "Fuck you Doc, don't you know when I'm throwing you a line in order to get your wife's permission to get out of that house and throw back a few brewskies?" He now launched forth with a total tirade.

We leave his apartment both pissed off at the situation and drive away into the night. Then inexplicably at a stop sign as I wait for the light to turn green the Judge unexpectedly gets out of the car and takes to walking into the night without a word. "Shit" I say aloud and wonder where he's going now and how much shittier can tonight possibly get?

I pulled over on the road leaving the car parked to follow him, and right at that moment he emerged from behind a concrete traffic pole drawing back his enormous left arm and clocked me right in the face with all the strength he could muster. Well, I didn't just have stars in my eyes, I had the whole milky way. I didn't just hear ringing in my ears I had a whole Wagner tour de force symphony. As I emerge from my daze I'm aware of the full not unsubstantial weight of his 6 foot 4 inch frame crushing my chest gently wiping blood from my nose urging, "Dude, you gotta become a better listener OK?" He went on and on … "Shit dude, you need to seriously work on your listening skills." We finally ended up at a tennis club where it was OK for me to be in sneakers and shorts looking for all the world like Bjorn Borg and concurrently fine for him to be looking like a disco king and "chick magnet" he'd left home determined to be that evening.

Shake your booty bitch!

A Solo Flight to Hollywood

The occasion was to receive a gold record. The Jazzman always picked up the cost of flights like these to avoid any appearance of impropriety with the record companies. A driver delivered me to an apartment somewhere in the Hills. I opened the fridge for a beer to find rows and rows of tiny vials, which I later discovered were filled with Amyl Nitrate. Uh oh, where's the Judge when I need him? This is new even for a boy like me who's been round the proverbial block a few times.

I caught up with a music producer friend and we settled into a high stakes game of backgammon, snorted some lines, hit some 'amie', then he whipped out salacious nude pictures of his current girlfriend who was on her way in from Dallas and was expected rather awkwardly to knock on the door at any moment. She was one of those girls who looked just as good naked as she did fully clothed.

As you might imagine I felt that I already knew her rather well before I met her though I did have a tough time (not surprisingly) looking her in the eye. My escort for the trip arrived shortly thereafter; she was a Hollywood jewel, smart witty and direct. She was second in command with her corporation. She lived splendidly across from Rudy Valee's home, which required us walking about 150 steps almost vertically to get to her perch, once there though our tête-à-tête was bliss.

The next morning sadly was an entirely different and deflating matter in many more ways than one. I was startled awake thinking that perhaps the Salvation Army was doing their charity runs in full orchestra. The sounds I was hearing though were not in fact the Salvation Army or any other sound of note but rather my date erupting into long continuous symphony of bellowing farts of every pitch, intensity, length and very soon every scent emanated stealth like from down the corridor throughout every inch of that house.

I begged to understand how it might be possible for someone so stunningly divine, this vision of loveliness, could possibly deliver such a caustic and disturbing cacophony of offensive sounds and smells.

We managed to move on beyond our ablution management issues and for a long period thereafter she cut a path to Florida to visit for over a year. In truth, for my part I was never able to fully recover from the morning of what could have been mistaken for a dramatic re-enactment of the Battle of Berlin both in toxicity and intensity of sound.

She called one day to say that she was going to marry a major motion picture actor. We never talked again but in one of her last appearances with her husband on the Johnny Carson show just before she died of breast cancer, she blew me a goodbye kiss, this time from her premier end, mercifully.

A pre-release of **Hotel California** *autographed by the Eagles and presented to Doc. It's one of only a few of Doc's collectibles to survive the destruction of his home during Hurricane Francis in 2004.*

Give the Drummer Some

Doc and the Judge, party dudes? Yes sir, tick that box and highlight it. The Mamma's were an eye popping four piece topless band I'd had some experience with and they were now on their way to sunny Ft. Lauderdale. Naturally as the Judge boasted a string of conquests rivaled only by Mozart's lothario Don Giovanni he'd have to be alerted.

As I'd intimately experienced the show myself in Detroit, I felt the Judge would want me to give him the appropriate notice to plan his stealth seduction moves to fulfill yet another of his fantasies. I told the Judge I'd spent some time with these "hotties" in Detroit, after confirming that they were indeed sizzling hot to which he bluntly drooled back, "Dude, do they fuck?" I retorted, "Judge come on you know it's their fantasy to fuck the 'uber dude' in every town and let's face it dude that's you, here, now." He didn't miss a beat barking back, "Shit Doc, you should know I've always wanted to fuck a topless rock 'n' roll band."

I assured him these girls could be conquered with lavishness and style, in short with good old fashioned courting. He instinctively understood courting even if it was merely a means to an end. He suggested we arrive on opening night in a limo and cleverly secure the front table for maximum exposure and impact. I told the Judge that the last time I saw the Mamma's the drummer was in fact happily ensconced and therefore mightn't be amenable to his considerable charms.

The others I offered were fair game and so we forged forth confidently shorting possible outcomes with the band. We agreed on $500 for each Mamma he had sex with and this wager doubled if he was able to snag the drummer too. He went to work on his charmarama offensive by sending the drummer a dozen long stemmed red roses while asking them all to keep an eye out for him adding mischievously he was often mistaken for Alice Cooper. He also suggested they might watch for him at the head table.

From the outset plans were off without a hitch however something about the project still didn't sit well with me – perhaps the multiples of moving parts and personalities. I simply couldn't put my finger on the issue, but something filled me with a general foreboding about the entire adventure.

On the night in question we arrived making our usual 'fashionably late' arrival at the club. As we worked our way through the throng in virtual pitch darkness toward the prized front table we unsettlingly discovered the room's filled to the rafters with men sitting close together, men unabashedly holding hands, men sitting cheek to cheek and with some men kissing passionately. Hmm, "unusual" note to self I venture. No matter, it's show time.

The lights go out, the spot light hits the stage, a rotund, over rehearsed announcer approaches the mike, his face illuminated a spooky Kabuki white. He grabs the mike and bellows in full voice, "Ladies and gentlemen for your pleasure we are proud to present for their first appearance on this stage 'Mammas Little Girls." He droned on and now I'm numb having realized my queasy feeling throughout this charade was letting me know I'd made a terrible mistake. This was wrong in so many ways, the Judge would lose face around town and he'd have my hide! "Ladies and Gentlemen please put your hands together and help me give a warm Ft. Lauderdale welcome to Mamma's Little Girls."

We find our table, sit down uneasily, I'm hissing at the Judge wanting to assure him there's been a terrible mistake, "Judge!" I call out above the throng for his attention, "They're cute, but these aren't the girls from Detroit." "What are you talking about dude, what the *&!@#$%&*" he lamented realizing the complexity of our exquisite dilemma. "Can't you see they're fat, ugly, hairy old men?" He hissed back, "Dude, I'm dead and if they don't kill me, I'll kill you." The look on the Judge's face is now morphing into abject terror.

The party however was on with a flourish. The Judge's red roses festoon the cheerful stage, more egregious than the roses and adding to his mounting horror we hear the band's drum roll and the leader announces while pointing clearly at the Judge, "Ladies and Gentlemen, tonight we're dedicating the entire show to the gorgeous gent at table one, ladies and gentleman a round of applause for our fabulous admirer." The Judge looks like he's going to be sick, pass out, or perhaps both.

The misery is by no means over for my friend or for that matter for me. In short order one by one Mamma's Little Girls jump off the stage and make their way over to sing at our table, dance at our table, sit and gyrate in our lap, and generally flaunt their old man titters in our face. Eeew dude! The Judge's immediate response is to dart a quick eye around the room with his single good eye scanning faces to assure himself he's not recognized by anyone as this excruciating and regrettable ordeal drags on, "This sort of thing destroys a studs reputation dude," he growled.

The finale of this extravaganza with the shit now hitting the proverbial fan comes as the drummer launches himself into the Judge's lap, canoodles coquettishly, playfully twisting the Judges' hair with his pretty pink drum sticks. Following this death by humiliation the Judge sheepishly endures the agony of having a long stemmed red rose slipped adoringly and sensually behind his right ear by this hirsute and apparently unstoppable freight train of affection in bad frock and bad pumps.

We knew we were screwed. We knew we'd be Mamma's Little Girls "boys" for the night. The Judge hissed, "I feel strangely cheap and slutty dude, what about you?" Shit Doc, think, I urge myself. "Kiss him and let's split," I tell the Judge. Meanwhile I remind myself to try to keep calm, think fast set out a plan for the Judge and me, and then plan to run for your life and for your virtue.

By now the Judge and I had acquired a veritable Rolodex full of police contacts. I escape on the pretense of going to the bathroom but actually run to make a desperate call to a friend we hoped was off duty that evening. I beg him to come and rescue us mostly from ourselves but also from these overzealous, amorous, belching songbirds.

He arrived quickly then professionally set to work performing better than we could have hoped for. In minutes it seemed, he was there in full uniform, with handcuffs and most importantly a stern no nonsense demeanor. He sought out then headed straight for management apologizing for having to disturb the show. He whispered to the manager they'd been tailing an Alice Cooper look alike and his accomplice friend who were both wanted in Florida for a string of crimes, who've been on the run for some time and police been tipped off they might be here tonight. Bingo!

He then turned to the audience, called for the mike and ordered the music cut then calmly told patrons, "Friends, we've found our 'men' here tonight." Some cheeky patron yelled out "I'm not at all surprised officer – men is all there ever is here any night," the crowd chortled at the comment and someone else chimed in with, "God, I hope I find my man here tonight officer, I love men in uniform," and purred like a tiger to suggest interest in the policeman. Our savior coughed uneasily and again apologized for the disturbance only this time to the patrons.

He cuffed the Judge and me roughly and then escorted us out to the unmarked police car waiting outside. He finally pushed us into the back and drove us away to safety.

On our way out of the club I clearly heard the lament of one of the band members wincing, "Oh why am I always falling for the bad boys Jimmy? Who'd have thought, I finally get a jock who does the flowers, spoils me rotten, sits front 'n' center transfixed by my performance and then bam, just like that the fuzz arrive and drag away my joy." My final vision was the keyboardist helpfully nodding and adding, "Oooh, I know and that cop was a beauty too wasn't he Jeff in that tight uniform and all?"

Who's a pretty girl then?

Transfixed by Lips

We took possession of the four rear seats in first class immediately. We being the Judge, Doc and two great friends of ours we'd bought along planning to take them backstage to meet Mick and the boys after the highly anticipated Rolling Stones concert we were on our way to see. As you'd expect, our foursome's party began before the plane ever left the tarmac. Minutes into the flight and we're now more than a little rowdy and in high spirits literally and figuratively.

A steward came forward and whispered quietly, "I want you boys to know the couple directly behind you in the front row of coach passed a note to the Captain reporting your unacceptable language and behavior. The wife told the captain one of you exposed himself while peeing in a cup and furthermore, the lady wants the incident reported to the police upon arrival at Jacksonville."

Well the flight droned on and what a "to-do" we landed into. We were asked to leave the plane first. "Uh oh dude," shot the Judge. An officer in full uniform met us and walked us off the plane pointing at us one by one calling, "Suspect 1 against the wall, suspect 2 against the wall, suspect 3 against the wall, suspect 4 against the wall now!" He continued on with his no nonsense efficiency ordering us, "Spread your legs, lean forward against the wall." For good measure he whispered, "You boys know you're in some serious trouble right?"

The Judge whispered to me, "I've got pot stuffed down my shorts dude." I said, "Sir, it's been a very long flight, my friend needs to get to the bathroom." "Yes, yes fine, just hurry back," he offers helpfully. Surprisingly all three of them rush to the toilet, flushing their goodies, and sullenly step back into line. Just at that time the couple who complained was approaching the lineup and we noticed the officer's tone toughen into barking orders at us as he patted us down.

When the couple had moved on he said, "Relax, boys. You're free to go, it's my job to check things out, you understand?" The Judge hissed, "Thanks, but I just lost my weekend down the toilet." The cop consoled him saying, "you'll find as much as you need around town … just go, have a good time and stay out of trouble." As we leave to make our way to the hotel and prepare to experience the ugliest band on earth, the Judge shares with me his new found admiration for police saying, "Shit dude I love the police and I respect all they do, hell, all they stand for. God Bless America."

We saw the couple in the rental car area and rushed to formation in preparation for their passing us on their way out of the airport. The Judge hissed urgently, "Dude here they come, everybody ready?" He was as excited as a naughty school boy over his wickedness, the excitement entirely overwhelming him. As the couple slowly drive toward us we all bend over from the waist bowing low and fulsome mooning them as we cheekily flap our 'ass'ets in the breeze to greet their car's approach. As in-synch as a rhythm and blues band, as in-synch as Fred Astaire and Ginger Rodgers, we are one in union flawlessly mooning and swooning our stuffy suburban nemesis.

The Judge bid them adieu memorably with an eloquent, "And don't ever do that again you boring fuckers." One of the other guys said we all fart a stinker in unison at them as they drive by but sadly this synchronicity wasn't so easy to cue. This was the first time I saw the Judge really and truly lose his cool. He turned to me and snapped, "That do-good witch and her spineless husband ruined my weekend Dude!"

His rage gathered steam and by the time we finally reached our hotel he set to stacking everything in the room toward the window fully intending to trash the room and throw everything out the window and 12 stories down. It was another urgent fantasy to execute and move on from. Apparently come hell or high water today was to be the day to tear up a hotel room in pure rock 'n' roll fashion.

He told me all the bands did it. Hell, even the Stones did it, urgently rationalizing to himself and hoping to convince me of the soundness of his plan with a throwaway. "Anyway dude, I gotta vent or I'll kill someone. That crazy housewife bitch from hell ruined my weekend and cost me my stash."

I caution him saying, "Judge, when a rock band destroys a room they've got handlers who cover charges, problems, incidentals - you know." He snapped back, "Well Doc, you're an officer of the company so go downstairs and alert management to what's about to happen, compensate them for their trouble." He pressed on with a flattery offensive, "You got it down dude, you know, go ahead handle me." Then he cajoled shamelessly, "Doc, just tell them my friend's manic depressive and he lost his meds (not entirely untrue) on the plane."

So, I sheepishly wander downstairs and find the manager to apprise him of the situation, "My friend's going to be fine when his medicine arrives but please go along with what may or may not happen in the interim." I assure him all costs would be covered. He seems like a reasonable man and asks helpfully, "Sir is he a danger to himself or others," to which I respond helpfully, "No, just let him toss a few things out the window rock 'n' roll style and he'll be OK."

I give the manager several hundred dollars and suggest he position a few workers where the side street met the main road to block any pedestrian traffic. I let him know the entire matter should be over in a few minutes and to sweeten the deal I grudgingly offer my tickets to the show which naturally seals the deal.

"Fine, fine just don't let the Judge throw the television out the window OK," he suggested. I'm sure in the back of his mind he wondered what kind of Judge flouts the law so blatantly? Perhaps one of those whacked out progressives from San Francisco famous for their idiotic approach and interpretation of constitutional law. And furthermore, how young is this Judge who thinks nothing of lifting and hurling a room full of heavy furniture out the window? I could see all these thoughts turning over in his mind.

He didn't know my Judge was 25 years old, hormonal, higher than any kite, 6' 4", mightily pissed off and with rage to purge. Mission accomplished, almost. I headed back into the room only to find the Judge has already torn the TV off the wall and is by window with it. Shit, all I could do was guide him where traffic below had been stopped in preparation for this dump from the 12th floor.

"Fire one! Look out below!" We barely hear the crash but the applause rippling up the side of the building is fulsome indicating a successful throw. In short order out went chairs, sofas, rugs, side tables and the final piece de resistance was the enormous king-sized mattress off the bed. The Judge was absolutely jubilant at have successfully playing out another fantasy.

When the car dropped us off at the stadium I asked the Judge to go ahead saying I'd catch up with him. After the show he had two questions, "Dude, who the hell was that old fart in your seat next to me throughout the show?" The Judge hissed at me "and where were you backstage?" I told him a feeling of charity overwhelmed me, so I gave the tickets to the old hotel manager.

I asked him, "So what are they like up close?" The judge soberly offered with a palpable shudder, "Dude, no doubt about it they've got to be the ugliest band in the world." I asked if he'd, "Got any autographs?" He quipped, "No. But I signed quite a few." He added in deep thought, "Let's walk dude and remember this day."

The next morning the mattress was still on the sidewalk with what appeared to be a homeless person curled up on it. Goodness seemed to follow wherever the Judge's path takes him. The following day the Judge did his standard swig of cold milk when he got up mid-afternoon while dispersing flower pedals in some psychedelic reverie over the mattress below.

Rock 'n' roll horizontal!

The Judge and WSHE staffer Cory James.

Gimme Shelter?

Our idea of charity was going directly to the problem, for example finding a young destitute child walking the streets in the projects, stopping and putting into his tiny hand a $20 bill and asking him to give it to his mother to buy him new shoes. We'd as easily buy and pass on a cold six pack of "girls" to a freak on the corner not because it was good for them but because we better than anyone knew how it was to be without. This is not to say we were uninvolved with established charities. We raised large amounts of money year after year for professional charities without question. However, we became jaded when we were shown that many charities kept up to 92% of the proceeds for the administration of the corporate arm of the company and that in fact as little as 8% would go to the needy it was being raised for and urgently needed by.

On one particular occasion the Judge and I worked to raise money for a telethon and we did in fact again raise over $50,000 only to learn after all our generosity and effort that the big charity it was being raised for was also keeping 92% of the revenue raised for administrative costs, with only 8% going to the charity. Needless to say we had another sudden and I believe understandable piss attack.

To this end the following year we bumped up our goal to a more ambitious minimum of $60,000 and we bought truckloads of mattresses, food, children's clothes, and so on and moved straight into the suburbs seeking out real need, not surprisingly and very sadly we found plenty. One day I hope to live in a world where the world of plenty will commit to cohabiting with equity and compassion with the world of want.

My dear mother would have been ashamed to be an American if she'd been alive today to be witness to the abject fraud perpetrated in the name of charity by some. She would have chided corrupt business practices in companies who unabashedly call themselves charity but only hide shamefully behind the apron skirts of decency while reaping obscene profits through the charitable sector guise.

No matter, on this day we press on and also remember the kindness and generosity of the people who freely gave up their time to help us load and unload the stuff – we threw in lots of "girls" for them. Life isn't perfect however, even when your personal agenda is above reproach.

We had packed my new white Jeep Cherokee with newly purchased clothes and headed to a very poor neighborhood in Miami. While we're stopped at a red light and as we wait for the light to turn green we spot a young boy 6 maybe 7, sitting on the curb holding some kind of can. Odd we both murmur and the Judge says, "Dude, why isn't that boy in school right now?" I press on with his concern, "In fact Judge, why aren't his parents taking better care of him?" Something told us he just didn't pass our charity filter, though we still handed him a twenty out the window. So, we press on with Judge and Doc's travelling charity mobile and as we move deeper into the neighborhood people are rude and violent. Now they are outright belligerent and begin to hurl rocks, cans, garbage, eggs, in short anything they could get their hands on quickly at my brand new car.

Soon we've moved beyond fretting over the car and we're starting to seriously fear for our safety. I speed up and start shooting into some back alleys hoping to find a way clear of the now seething throbbing mob. We finally arrive exiting into a large shopping center parking lot where I get out looking for signs that might have provoked this venom. What we find spray painted in bold black letters right across the curb side of my white car is "We hate niggers!" That kid on the curb, we both had a Eureka moment of the very worst kind!

Not allowing ourselves to be perturbed by this setback we surmised he didn't appreciate charity – but why did he take the money? Perhaps it's a daily trick in the "hood" to keep visitors out. Either way, it worked. I wondered if this kid would've been sitting on this curb on this school day if Martin Luther King had not been taken from us a decade earlier. I wonder whether this child's parents might have been more proud to teach him aspiration, righteous hope, pride and self actualization.

We drove on to Miami Beach where there were a lot of elderly forgotten people, some of whom knew they'd been placed there by families to keep them out of sight and out of mind. How could Grandma not enjoy living in Miami Beach with people her own age, they easily assuaged their heavy conscience.

Generally we were told by staff in the facilities, and the elders themselves when approached that the problem was that often grandma or granddad was not properly funded for food, clothing needs or for bills. We found a group of elderly men and women gathered around a bus bench. We asked if they could use some of the new clothes we had in the vehicle. Oh yes dear was their unanimous reply.

We heard some say they would take them to a second hand shop and exchange them for money, others said they'd ship them home to grandkids, most however seemed overcome with the kindness and the opportunity presented to have a change of clothes that were in good order.

Mission accomplished "dynamic dudes."

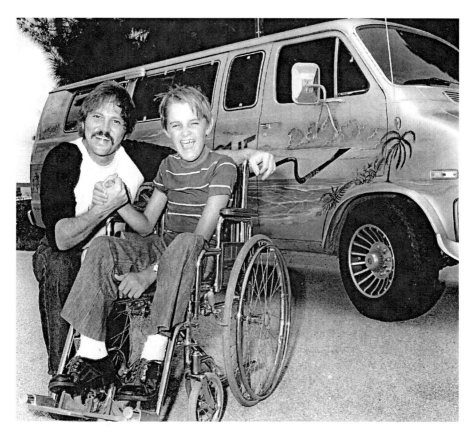

Doc with Muscular Dystrophy Poster Child.

Doc and the Judge

Teddy Bears

A standing challenge between the Judge and me was to see who could score the most teddy bears from the gamers at carnivals. On this one night in particular, we split up and knowing the stakes were high each of us was fully aware of the lengths the other might be prepared to go to for an assured win. So, I set off in one direction with a roll of fresh $20 bills exploding in my pocket while the Judge took off in the other direction, candy in one pocket, a few joints in the other.

I struck out totally with my first twenty but when I doubled it to forty I scored a two foot pink furry rabbit. It took me forty $1.00 shots with the basketball to finally hit three in a row to win the prize. The carnie said that the third shot rimmed out, which I didn't see in my exuberance, for another $20 though he agreed to let me take home the hot pink bunny.

Now I was anxious to search out the Judge to show off my hot pink trophy. On my way back I spotted what appeared to be a cart like those delivering hay to horses rumbling my way with a load of teddy bears. There were seven bears of various sizes and colors stuffed into the cart and the Judge had the largest one under his arm. "How'd you do dude?" He asked smugly. "I did fine but it looks like you did something illegal," I shot back.

He said he'd scored with the candy, and the ancient culture of barter. "No money changed hands so nothing improper happened, dude," he protested rather emphatically then he added bitingly, "How'd you score that puny rabbit?" "I scored this beautiful teddy through athletic skill. I paid forty dollars for forty shots at the basket and all I had to do was make three shots in a row," I retorted with derision. "And?" He urged. "Well, I had lots of two and outs but by the end I almost swished all three." He asked me suspiciously… "What do you mean, almost?" "The carnie said that the third shot rimmed out as I was looking away in the midst of my overzealous exuberance," I confessed. "How'd you get the bear?" He ventured. "I negotiated to buy the bear for another $20."

The Judge pondered a moment then suggested, "Dude, that's not cool." He went on in mock disappointment, "Using cash under the table to score a prize is illegal, you know that! This is a barter house and I hope you've learned something from this. Trade your $20's for candy. Know your audience. Throw your rabbit on the cart and let's get out of this fucking barn."

I never thought I'd live to see the day when the Judge was in a position to chide me about ethics! Can you imagine him advising me on ethics? Huh - who'd have imagined that? When we got to our natural home needless to say every waitress in the bar got a teddy bear that night and one got a bunny. Gotcha!

Two Time Loser

The Judge was fast gaining a reputation as a great golfer. He was always on the top of the lists for all the large charity tournaments. He stayed away from purse tournaments to protect his amateur status. Naturally, there were always calls for matches with some club champion or hustler who wanted to beat the Judge. The word was you could beat him by teeing it up around 11 a.m., which was three hours earlier than he normally gets up and just five hours after he'd gone to bed.

I always got him there just in time to get out of the car and mosey on to the first tee. Grunting, groaning, he'd slip the Kool out of his mouth and place it onto the grass as he affected a troubling cough. He'd always cough more the nastier his opponent seemed, then he'd spit on the grass as he approached his opponent if he took a more particular distaste to them. This all contrived to give his opponent the impression that this adversary was sickly and quite probably suffering the remains of a hangover which would surely affect his game.

Meanwhile I'd get to work setting up a cart, a cooler filled with beer and water which he'd occasionally dip into to moisten his towel to wash his bad eye once he'd removed the eye patch to tend to it. Only after this ritual would he begin to approach his opponent to shake his hand and thereby start the game.

I'd helpfully send out feelers explaining the Judge played scratch and would accept bets from anyone with a 5 or less handicap. I'd announce it was eighteen holes match play with "carries" and that in the event of a rainout bets owed at that point stood. The bet was a dime a hole (a dime was $100.00). The Judge was like a stealth panther around his prey and always delighted in finding a quiet moment to whisper helpfully to his unsuspecting prey, "Feel free to press when you're nervous."

Other rules were always set out fast and furious and on this day the Judge has laid out his playing conditions always having been a stickler for observing those sacred golf rules. He adds, "Gimme putts are OK, you can choose to forfeit a hole and move on. Bets should be paid within 24 hours of the match." He wound up with "all rules now being established and clear, tee it high and let it fly!"

We're playing on this day against an irritating mid-20's, pissant, playboy type whose claim to fame is playing on the golf team of a northern university and that his father was a member of Doral. I drove the Judge's cart, the playboy had a very young girl whom he ordered to drag around his bag and wipe his brow. The Judge never allowed anyone to carry his bag nor wipe anything.

The Judge accepted honors and with his right hand twitching and shaking he managed to stick the tee upright in the ground. He wasn't nervous, just sleepy he liked to explain. After a practice swing he hit the ball three hundred yards down the middle of the fairway. Nice shot everyone said, the Judge grunted and gave me a half wink. The playboy hits his ball very close to the Judge's. They both hit 9 irons onto the green, the Judge about 15 feet away and the playboy about 10. The Judge makes an amazing putt for birdie and the playboy's putt comes up short. "We've got ourselves one here Doc," he said, "this'll be fun." I knew exactly what he meant.

The Judge's tee shot on the 2nd hole found the fairway bunker, playboy was down the middle. The Judge was the only golfer I've known who could fake a bad swing; he lived to lull his opponents into a false sense of security and in so doing create an opportunity to pounce just like the panther. After all, it's all about the kill. But I digress, the Judge hit about a foot behind the ball which gave it just enough lift to clear the bunker and land in the fairway. The playboy's second shot was on the green 10-15 feet from the pin. The Judge's third shot was on the green but way short. He two putted for a bogie, the playboy made par. Match even.

The Judge shows perfect form in the sand.

The playboy hits his normal straight shot off the third tee and the Judge again pushed it into the bunker. As if following a script, the Judge hit the same type of sand shot lying two in the fairway. The playboy won the hole and is 1 up going into the 4th hole, which was a par three surrounded by water. The playboy birdies the hole; the Judge knocks it in the water. Down 2 going into the 5th hole, sand on both sides and a canal running down the right side of the fairway.

The playboy reminded the Judge that this was the 2nd handicap hole and you can see why with all that sand and water. The Judge broke a long silence by saying, "shit, I'm nervous, I think it's time to press." Also, in case this match gets out of hand, can we agree to any bet being doubled at anytime. We're now down $200 on the first bet with a second bet of $100. At the turn the Judge was up +3-+5-+3+1 or $1,200. He had a couple of shots of tequila at the bar, ordered a cold ham and cheese sandwich with butter, mayo, and mustard and met me on #10.

I was surprised that the Judge had gone for the kill so early. He said that he didn't like the way the playboy was treating his caddie and felt that being humbled in front of her might help her in some way. The playboy only won a couple of holes on the back nine, backed off on his presses, and dropped about $2000 to the Judge. He was already building excuses that it might take him a couple of days to come up with the money. The Judge told him not to worry and even asked if he and his girlfriend would like to join us in a couple of weeks for a road trip to Vail for some skiing. He was told that we would each bring girlfriends and would divide the costs of the RV, lodging, and gasoline three ways. All agreed.

The playboy's wager debt was only mentioned once, and not by him. We were a day or so into the drive west, the playboy was asleep in the master suite and his girlfriend/caddie was sitting next to me in the co-captains seat. She noticed that I took my eyes off the road and looked at her with a shrug of the shoulders when she asked if the playboy had paid his bet to the Judge. "Don't expect it," she said. "He'll find a way to get out of paying. The money I brought with me for the trip is missing from my wallet, I think he took it while I was sleeping last night, watch him."

Every time we stopped for gas the playboy slept through, rushed to the pay phone for an urgent business call or roosted on the toilet. The point is he was always mysteriously ready as soon as he heard the engine turn on, ready to hit the road and in the knowledge that the bill had been paid! We were beginning to wonder what it might take to shake "Ebenezer Scrooge's" money loose.

He occasionally contributed to the drive when he liked to sit high in the captain's chair in boxer shorts while the caddie subserviently gave him sponge baths and massages with scented oils. He demanded pedicures and manicures; all this she was expected to do from the crawl space under the steering wheel to reach him. He constantly barked abuse, cursed using foul language just as he had on the golf course a few weeks earlier. There was no discomfort to him in our being witness to the whole disgraceful affair. The Judge said soberly, "Doc, he's just an outright asshole but I just don't know which one's sicker, him or her?"

As we entered the lodge the playboy stopped us and said that he had called ahead to arrange for a separate room for the two of them next to ours. He said they needed some private time together, and that he didn't think it necessary that we share in the additional costs. What??? We saw very little of them over the next few days except when they came around for lunch or dinner. We did hear a lot from their room however … lots of noise including furniture being thrown around, shouting from the playboy and upsetting crying and whimpering from the caddie.

We noticed when they dropped in for food that the caddie seemed to be wearing more and more heavy makeup. She looked disheveled and out of sorts. She was looking less and less like the girl we met on the golf course weeks earlier. The night before our departure was the worst. This time the sounds of crying and moaning were accompanied by screaming and pleading.

A knock on their door was answered by the playboy standing in his underwear holding an almost empty bottle of Jack Daniels. The huge Judge could easily see over the playboy, spotting the caddie sitting in a large cushioned chair. She appeared half out of it but raised her hand to wave as if to say that everything was OK. The playboy apologized for all the noise saying that the two of them had gotten carried away with frisky sex games. He promised the noise would stop and they'd be packed and ready to leave at the scheduled time of 7:00 am the following morning. The caddie was the last to board the RV, we were all surprised to see her shrouded in a scarf, another cravat around her neck clearly fluffed to the maximum to cover most of her face. It was obvious that she'd been crying and more than obvious she was terribly beaten up.

The playboy was already perched on the bed and announced we ought to stop for gas, naturally neither he nor anyone else expected him to part with a penny for gas or provisions required to proceed with our trip homeward bound. Our girls asked the caddie to go to the gas station's bathroom with them where our worst fears are confirmed. The caddie's scarf covered her beautiful but beaten young face. She looked as though she was the loser in a knock down, drag out, street brawl.

We saw that she could barely draw breath through her blood caked nostrils, her left eye swollen shut and most disturbingly we couldn't miss what were vividly clear handprints about her neck. She said, finally trusting us enough to tell us everything, including the fact that he'd been beating her since our arrival at the lodge but that it got progressively worse with last night having been the very worst. She pleaded with us not to call the police as she was underage. This was what he held over her and so as she'd run away he knew her mother was unaware of her whereabouts.

She asked to be allowed to sit in the master bedroom alone saying she'd like to attempt to heal her body hoping the swelling might diminish before we made it back home. The Judge woke the playboy thumping a golf club across the bottom of his feet holding off on exhibiting all rage and contempt for this miserable human garbage. We both sat on the bed and laid down the new rules slowly and succinctly for the turd.

We warned him he'd be wise to shut up and listen. He fell apart as all cowards who are abusive to those weaker than themselves do. We stipulated he was not, we repeated for emphasis, "Not to talk to, touch, or go near the girl, furthermore, the master suite's exclusively hers." We added, "Pay up now for your portion of the trip and share your expenses from here on in."

It was as though he'd been physically winded by the confrontation and we guessed no one had ever stood up to him before? How so though, the fellow was absolutely odious! He had no choice but to agree, begging us not to call the police saying the whole thing was a misunderstanding, prattling on that the young girl was a willing participant who was eager for their rough games.

As for the money situation, and covering his share he said, "I'm low on cash right now, but if we stop at the next town I'll wire father for money." What a shocker dude! First, he wants to find a country club where he'd shower, freshen up so he'd be neat and clean for his bank meeting for the money transfer. He'd call his father from the club, this was my first experience with a pathetic, 25-year-old, loser who neither pays his bills nor has done an honest day's work in his life. Some people feel they are such precious cargo for the world that they need to be carried as a precious burden might be, with the same gravitas and deep veneration for the provenance. This piece of excrement was a piece of work but nothing about him was good, just, or inspired. What a stinking miserable piece of garbage.

We turned off the freeway at the next ramp leading us into a sizeable town where we expected there'd be a country club. The playboy bellowed instructions to the caddie about what clothes he needed from the bedroom. When she opened his duffle bag she found his wallet inside which he'd cunningly stuffed in there hoping to make a complete getaway while we waited for him to have a shower and discharge his growing debts to us.

As soon as he stepped out she ran to us in the front of the RV whispering, "I've got his wallet." Think fast Doc. Inside was an assortment of credit cards, gas cards, hotel cards, driver's license, and about $1700 in cash in one pouch and another $500 stuffed in a side pocket which the young girl explained was hers but which he'd refused to return to her. I scribbled a terse note wrapping it around his American Express card which read, "No reason to call the police, we have the victim with us and she's safe. As for the money, it doesn't begin to cover what you owe, but let's call everything even … including the bet. Adios, you sick mother fucker!"

The young girl ran into the Country Club lobby with his wallet (having had the presence of mind to remove his driver's license) while he showered, she told the manager she'd found it outside and as it probably belonged to one of their patrons and so would he please try to get it back to its owner. Away we went!

On the road again, we found country music on the radio, did the Texas two-step in the living room of the RV laughing all the way to the Louisiana border. The young girl blossomed, genuinely beaming for the first time, no doubt relieved to have escaped her nightmare with bodily harm only – we sensed and apparently she sensed also that things could have been fatal for her if we'd not intervened.

We discovered her smile more and more as her confidence grew, she flashed a dazzling smile we'd not seen during the early part of their travel with us, as it turned out not at all surprisingly in retrospect. This tender young soul was coming to life.

She was a young girl who now felt she'd like to fill in all the blanks for us and let us know how she and the playboy came to be together. She said she'd met the playboy at a bar a few days before she'd caddied during the Judge's match with him; she'd been living with him from the first day of their chance meeting. She'd experienced some rage from him but nothing like what had recently transpired.

She confided this was a jumble of firsts for her i.e. first trip with anyone, her first time running away from home. She told us how glad she was that she never told him her real name nor where she lived. She asked if we'd mind going a little out of our way to drop her off at her aunt's house in Okeechobee, Florida where her body could heal before her mother saw her again. Done, we gave her the cash he'd taken from her, and gave her all his cash too.

The two of them are a dim, distant memory and needless to say from that point onward we chose golf matches and traveling companions more discerningly. May bad karma follow this human garbage for the rest of his miserable life, finally may he have daughters, whose welfare compels him to prostrate himself humbly before God, that He might protect them from vermin such as himself throughout their vulnerable lives.

Tee him high and let him fly!

Georgia on My Mind

Neither the Judge nor I ever attempted any analysis of our friendship. I believe as with all mysteriously and splendidly wonderful things, it too "just was." People in great relationships I imagine, have no need of analyzing or dissecting the perfect oneness of their situation. It's just as it is, forever evolving to a newness which defies you to pick a peak since just when you think you're there, and now gently preparing yourself to plateau at the magnificence you've achieved you slide onward ever more toward a deeper, higher more spiritual plane which leaves you even more expectant for the possibility of tomorrow.

"Yee Haw! Dude we're on a road trip to Atlanta to break in my brand new 'little red corvette,'" I teased the Judge. The car was a gift from the Jazzman for growing our radio station beyond everyone's wildest expectations. He knew the Judge and I had done it together but he always passed the lion's share of the accolade to me. He knew however that I was the fortifier in the duo and so though the Jazzman recognized the freedom he'd given us to party, travel, come and go as we please on our relentless pursuit of perfection but that this very chemistry had led us here.

We'd work all night on a concept then disappear on a road trip to listen to it on the radio uninterrupted so we could hear it as the listening audience would and from that perspective honestly critique our idea. Our success rate was really quite remarkable and the big ideas generally resulted in the obligatory road trip both to work out any remaining details as well as to celebrate our genius.

On this particular trip to Atlanta the only clothes we took were what we could physically squeeze into the car. So our maiden voyage with the Vette included clothes that could be stuffed into the golf bag which was the only one taken and the bag was then tied to the luggage rack on the new car. The T top had been removed and tucked away behind the seats and so space was at a premium on this trip.

The Judge's gift to Doc to go along with his new corvette. The clubs and bag are like new and Doc still plays the sand wedge.

To congratulate me in his inimitable way the Judge bought me a set of the newly released Jack Nicklaus VIP clubs from the 3 iron right through to the sand wedge, adding a driver, and the three, four, and five woods naturally all made of persimmon. He said, "Every new corvette should come with a new set of golf clubs dude, congratulations." I still play the sand wedge. The bag and entire set of clubs are still with me, close by, as is the Judge whispering, "Tee it high and let it fly, dude."

The Judge drove on this trip saying he wanted to give the "Vette" its first road test. The speedometer said it would do 140 mph so the Judge wanted to be sure I hadn't been sold a lemon. On this drive I had flashbacks of that first night I met the Judge with him driving 100 mph up and down the rows of orange groves in Ft. Lauderdale. I reminded myself that we would survive this high speed run as we did that first one years ago through those lush orange groves of South Florida on that memorable first day when the Judge and I met. In fact in hindsight after the long run on the four-lane freeways the exhilaration of flying past row after row of endless orange groves was beautifully moving and soothing on both eyes and soul.

Even today, I placated myself, there really was nothing much to worry about as long as he kept the car pointing straight. However as he ran it up to max speed while leaning his head out the window screaming, "Rock 'n' roll" with his unruly black mop making it impossible for him to see ahead, I'll come clean and confess I was more than a little uneasy. He would occasionally remind me to keep an eye on the golf bag to be sure it was still up there. "What the fuck?" What on earth did he think I could do if the bag was no longer there at 140 mph???

As we passed the exit for Macon Georgia about 5 a.m. I reminded the Judge that my hometown was about 40 miles west of the freeway and he knew my mother and father still lived there. The Vette went from about 80 mph to a full stop within seconds. The Judge backed up weaving and bobbing about ¼ mile to the exit we had passed seconds earlier. He said, "Dude, we're going to show Buck and Flo your new Corvette; I'll bet Flo is already making biscuits!"

And so we shortly arrive in Thomaston, Georgia just before sunrise doing about 90 mph. I noticed lights turning on in houses as he squealed the tires around the little town and headed up Highway 19 toward Buck and Flo's. We were the Dukes of Hazard before that show was ever a concept let alone a runaway hit.

We drive up and the carport light comes on. I noticed Buck peering through the kitchen curtains holding his 22 rifle. The Judge blew the horn and I starting shouting, "Daddy, it's us . . . me and the Judge!" "You boys shouldn't sneak up on people like this . . . somebody could've been hurt," he said. "What kind of car is that you're driving son?" Was his next question. "The Judge will show it to you after breakfast, let's eat," I suggested helpfully.

The Judge loved my mother Flo's southern cooking. He knew he'd always get eggs over easy, grits with lots of butter and gravy, a slab of bacon and hot fluffy homemade biscuits dripping with butter, which he would have open faced smothered with cold Cairo Cane Syrup topped off with an icy glass of cold milk. The Judge was dining with good American Folk and having great southern cuisine at Florine and Buck's.

By mid-morning the word was out that Doc and the Judge were in town. One by one folks start arriving bringing their cameras taking happy snaps of the city slickers and the fancy car. As the crowd grew, the Judge begged, "Stay close dude I can't understand a word they're saying," which cracked me and my parents up. We mimicked him at that moment of sheer terror and had chuckles about his fear for years afterwards, they loved the Judge.

One comment was, "Yeah, we heard down at the firehouse that you guys made quite an entrance into town this morning even waking up the preacher hours before church on this Sunday and day of our Lord." Apparently this was sacrilegious but neither the Judge nor I had any notion of the fact.

Some asked the Judge why he wore a patch over one eye, and others inquiring, "That's your real hair then, is it?" Mothers with daughters of marrying age twittered incessantly, "Doc and the Judge, those rascals are rich don't you know." Most comments and questions though were restricted to the new Corvette. Somebody said, "They say it's Doc's new car, that it was given to him at work," to which a skeptic snapped, "Now why would some dang fool do a thing like that fer?"

The Judge held a golf clinic in the backyard with my new Nicholas VIP's. I hope that day with the Judge inspired some young and old kids to take up the game even though it was obvious most were swinging a golf club for the first time.

It was decided that we would all meet for supper at my grandmother's house (Buck's mother). There'd be a southern feast of fried chicken, mashed potatoes, cornbread, beans and tasty tomatoes fresh out of the garden. Word got out that there was the drinking of beer and maybe even the unmistakable smell of marijuana out back in grandma's yard, and even her son Buck was seen with a beer in his hand. It was a good thing we'd already eaten because all hell was about to break loose.

Grandma was having a heart attack. She was lying in the middle of the floor grasping her chest, her head heavily draped with wet towels to calm her fever. "The ambulance's on its way Buck," someone soothed father. Another party conspiratorially whispered to the Judge and I outside, "Don't worry she's just fine, I've seen her fake a heart attack before when she felt she needed to regain attention. You boys get on the road, promise you'll come back through here on your way home."

With that sage advice we hightail it out of the drive (with me driving this time because I knew the back roads) just as the ambulance pulled into Grandma's house. Our departure apparently resulted in grandma's remission and miraculous recovery. She was sitting upright in a chair sipping lemonade when the emergency personnel stepped up to the house. They took her blood pressure, assuring everyone she's as fit as a fiddle and that she's fine.

They cautiously diagnosed the problem as, "Too much excitement with Grandma having her beloved grandson home." It did seem to the Judge and me as outsiders that an inordinate amount of time, energy, personnel had been gone through for such a "dang loose diagnosis dude."

She lived for many years after that, in fact she was well into her nineties when she finally passed and ultimately when it was time to go she knew and simply announced that it was time to go to bed and died peacefully within minutes of lying down. At a break stop the Judge says, "Thanks Doc. Dude, this was an interesting day anthropologically speaking, you southerners are eccentric."

Cat Scratch Fever

There was a straight line between Detroit music and South Florida. We were always first to play albums right out of the box by Seger, Nugent, Brownsville Station and the like. Seger and I split the gate more than once at Our Lady Gate of Heaven Church in Detroit.

My last show before leaving for South Florida in fact was with a three-way split. Seger took 50% of the gate, the church and I split the other 50%. The gym was packed. My final money settlement in Detroit was upstairs with me squaring 25% of the door, many final goodbyes and hasty hugs then a mad dash out the door for Ft. Lauderdale. I walked into a large poker game with the priest sitting at a full table of players. Since we'd already agreed on the ticket count I quickly left pocketing my earnings leaving some tithe for the needy with the Father and thoughtfully allowing him to continue on with his red hot winning hand.

I first saw Ted Nugent at the Atlanta Auditorium where he'd opened for Jimi Hendrix. They sold out two shows. The intermission between the two shows seemed unusually long. I later learned that Hendrix was telling his handlers backstage that Nugent was not to appear for the second show. Young Ted was simply doing what he always did, grinding the guitar, but on this particular night Hendrix felt upstaged and was unhappy about it. Nugent won this night without ever knowing there was a competition.

The Judge and I were on the annual calls of reminders to vote for groups in the various music polls. *Cat Scratch Fever* was Nugent's latest release. As late as a few weeks after the release the Judge and I were still uncertain about the album which obviously meant we weren't playing it. Nugent called and menacingly hissed, "I'm in town, and I promise if you don't start playing the album today I'll come over and break your fucking neck. What's wrong with you, dude!?" It was all in 70's rock 'n' roll fun; let's just say a quick and mutual accommodation was found after we thought long and hard for a second.

Doc and the Judge

Rock 'N' Roll Marathons

Warner Brothers called to see if we would do a promotion for a new group called KISS. We were told that some stations were playing the sound of a "kiss" and taking the ninth caller to win a KISS album. The Judge and I said let's think about it, let's not be hasty and so we listened to the album at my apartment over a couple of "girls."

"Shit, this is terrible," the Judge said, followed quickly with, "I do like the name though dude." He pressed on "KISS sounds intriguing, what do you say Doc?" We played around with a few ideas. We decided to first record the sound of a kiss and reverse it to see if anyone could identify the sound. The first person to identify the sound received the new KISS album. It took two days to get a winner. The next faze was to find the best "kiss in public" for a trip to Atlanta to see KISS live.

The winning answer came from a girl who was leaving her current female lover to catch a plane to meet up with her boyfriend, present fiancé and soon to be husband! Whew, the Judge and I shrugged it off to a sign of modernity with interpersonal connections being as complicated and convoluted as the rest of life.

The third and final component of the competition was to be a kissing contest. The Judge and I had come up the "Marathon Kiss Competition" whereby the longest kiss would win cash and prizes, and far more than anyone ever imagined, including appearances on the Johnny Carson Show, Mike Douglas, Show, What's My Line, and interviews in the mainstream media and entertainment publications. The contest was restricted to members of the opposite sex. We had a few couples of the same sex show up to register but it was illegal in the terms of our authorization for the contest for us to allow them to participate. A "carpenter kitty" and his soul mate endured for 92+ hours. The Judge and I sat in the bar and watched the CBS News trucks drive up to feed the story back for the evening news with Walter Cronkite.

Kiss and tell dude!

Betcha!

The Judge and I bet on everything from golf, baseball, basketball, boxing, hockey, tennis, who'd get laid first, right through to who'd be married the most times; I'm sure you get my drift. Naturally and as always as Chief Manager I kept a running total of money owed in a little black book where bets were reconciled and settled at the end of every year. To make things more interesting they were often seasoned with a double or nothing coin flip or roll of the dice on New Year's Eve.

Over all our years of this crazy competitiveness however the little black book shows I was up $50 over the Judge. But really the big bucks flowed at the annual Super Bowl party. We conceived the event as assiduously as a wedding planner would. We'd set down portable seating stands which were borrowed for a nominal fee from a local school and we liked this because in this way education became another charitable endeavor we backed.

Next AstroTurf was laid over the living room carpet to offer the complete stadium experience for the super bowl festivities that would follow. Tickets to the party were then available to select people with $100.00 buying an assigned seat in the stands in front of the big TV, with catering for the day an added bonus. A $50 purchase bought standing room in another room with a regular size TV. By halftime everyone gathered in front of the large TV. Another $500 per person was required for the betting pool. Each ticket holder was given a large card where they marked their pick of the bets which indicated the relative value of each. All cards had to be turned in before kick-off and there was another round of betting for the second half for those playing catch up, here the bets doubled.

The bet selections included but were not always limited to: coin toss winner, whether the winner would choose to kick or receive, whether there would be a return on the kickoff, which team received the first penalty, who would call the first time out, who would receive the most penalty yards in each quarter, who would fumble first and most, who would be leading at the end of each quarter, who would gain the most yards per quarter, who'd gain the most total yards for the game, who'd punt first and last, who would kick the longest field goal, which team would have the longest run from scrimmage, which team would have the most passing yards, and ultimately who'd win the game.

The tie-breaker would be the person who guessed the closest result to the winning score. A large scoreboard was visible for all to monitor their own and others standing in the rankings so they could plan and adjust their ongoing strategy. The person with the most points got 50% of the pool with payouts for the top-ten.

It was a huge "pay day" for the winner with a lot of strewn bodies to trample on one's way out the door the following morning if one had an urgent "can't wait" kind of appointment. It was common knowledge that the Judge and I took 10% off the gross which we in turn "prized" to the most enthusiastic female reveler of the party. Naturally, off-duty police officer friends were admitted gratis and they got a front row seat though from time to time they'd need to be called on in their official capacity to keep the peace.

Then there was the bet on who could come up with the most creative way to get some attention for the station during the Super Bowl between the Steelers and the Cowboys at the Orange Bowl in 1979. The rules were simple; there was only one. Gain the most attention without putting anyone in peril. Ha! The Judge presented his idea of having a plane "sky write" the station's call letters all day long. I don't think the Judge spent much time coming up with this idea.

I came back with something a bit more grandiose and would require exacting coordination. No problem. One of our drinking pals, who enjoyed a full replay of our antics every time we returned from a trip, flew bombing raids in World War Two. He himself, a widower who was on his last days of a long battle with lung cancer, said that hanging out with Doc and the Judge made him feel young again, and took his mind off his inevitable fate. His name was Red.

Here's the plan. At the precise moment of the opening kickoff to start the game Red would swoop down in his refurbished B-25 bomber and drop 10,000 footballs onto the field. The vision of 10,000 footballs carrying the inscription, "She's Only Rock 'n' Roll Bitch" falling from the sky as the receiving team looked up trying to decide which one was the real game ball was too much to resist. Hell, we knew that the cameras would capture the event; there wouldn't be time for the cameras to cut away. It would become an instant worldwide story that would be replayed on television forever, and no one would be hurt … and after all, it was just a football game. The fallout? We figured whatever the charges would be easily balanced on the other side of the enormous publicity we would receive. As for Red, he would likely lose his pilot's license, which he didn't see as a problem since he only had a short time to live anyway. And, he said, "Shit boys, I'll go out in flames just like the good old days! I'm in!"

Sadly for Red, and in hindsight, thankfully for us Red passed away four months before the game. Had we pulled it off, in 1979 we would have been seen simply as trouble makers; today we would be seen as terrorists.

Doc won the wager.

Doc and the Judge

Ten Years After

The decade of the 70's is coming to an end. I've blown past the age of thirty and the Judge is fast approaching his own age of reckoning. The drugs are gone. The Judge's now sipping Dewar's and soda and I will occasionally have a margarita or one of those fancy drinks that are served with a small umbrella. I've adopted a fitness program which includes jogging two miles every morning and two every afternoon. The Judge says I've turned into a "wuss" over night.

Jazzman and I are meeting with computer programmers to begin transitioning the business into the brave new world. The Judge wasn't interested. He had a unique talent of doing things "on the fly" and couldn't see himself partnering with a machine, which to him would stifle his creative genius.

We will still catch up three or four times a week at our favorite watering holes: Stan's, Mai Kai, Trysting Place, and so on and our conversations now seem to focus more on the past than the future. "Where's it all going Doc," he would ask. He once asked me to repeat that stupid thing I said to him during our first meeting, "We will never again be what we were yesterday, and tomorrow not what we are today." "Shit dude, I think that thin thread is frayed and about to break."

Tomorrow looms on the horizon.

Doc and the Judge Call it Quits

Doc and the Judge are growing in different directions, not growing apart just in different directions. Like in football, the Judge still wanted to put the pads on everyday and knock it around with the youngsters, and Doc envisioned coaching and moving on into the front office.

"Tomorrow" is arriving, and I must say in looking back the Jazzman's belief in me directed his kind and thoughtful orchestration of my transition. Knowing that the sale of the stations was imminent and that the new owners would likely bring in their own management staff he put me on a business regimen that could be likened to getting an MBA in record time.

The Jazzman's advice started with, "Lose the jeans, the long hair and the eye popping rhinestone boots son." Next he sagely whispered, "Better get yourself a few suits, better get real fine ones!" Our one-on-one meetings focused on demystifying the balance sheet, the P&L, the top line to the bottom line and everything in between. He wanted to be sure I understood it all.

Meetings with record reps for me were replaced with trips to Washington imbedded in long arduous meetings with FCC attorneys. Other new commitments now included trips to national advertisers to learn how business was done at that level. His final mentor action and one that has stood me in

Doc ... circa 1985.

good stead ever since was including me on lecture circuit tours then arranging for me to lecture at some of the top colleges about broadcasting as part of their Communications curriculum. He was polishing me up for graduation and more movingly making me in his own image.

As for the Judge, he continued on his path of brilliance in programming and music selection. He too was being prepared for his future, the heir apparent of his father's business, whenever it transpired after the sale of the Ft. Lauderdale properties.

It was the Jazzman's greatest contribution to his apprentice, and eldest son. He was preparing us both to move out of the frat house and into the boardroom. He knew we were ready. Almost a decade had passed since that first day with the Jazzman and that infamous night with the Judge on the roof of the radio station. Many inspired years of partnership and hard work had passed in what seemed like a moment. And here we were. It was 1980.

I move on as Director of Sales for a company in West Palm Beach, then two years later as President of an operation in Virginia. By now I'm in a new marriage and we've adopted a beautiful child from India. Jazzman and the Judge take a couple of years off to justly unwind and draw breath then buy a group of radio stations in Illinois.

I'm flabbergasted to learn the Judge has whacked off his long hair and now he too is beginning to take on greater and greater responsibilities for his father. The Jazzman calls me frequently to ask specific questions about business such as advice on financing deals, advice on how to improve bottom line performance, recruit sellers, control expenses and so on. Secretly I had no doubt that rather than calling for advice, he was calling in fact to rate the master's apprentice. He was generous enough to treat my responses as if each session was a learning experience for him.

The Judge is growing up.

We should all be fortunate enough to find a mentor like the Jazzman.

The Judge is Dead

Often we seem to sense tragedy coming before the news actually reaches us. It's like a built-in trigger to release some of the shock beforehand to help buffer our emotions and prepare us for the inevitable calamity that lies ahead. My mother always said she knew her daughter wasn't returning to her room even before the doctors came to deliver the tragic news of her death.

I've heard mothers and fathers of fallen soldiers also say that they knew their son or daughter had been killed in action long before the unmarked car arrived at the curb with military personnel there to deliver the devastating news. I knew 6 months before my father died that his time was limited when he asked on Thanksgiving Day one year, "Let's you and I stop smoking, what do you say, I'm not feeling real good these days."

The Judge's mother was sitting by the window reading on the rainy night when she noticed a strange car pull up in front of her house. She knew something bad had happened to her son.

When I returned home from work that afternoon on my first day of a new job and found my mother, wife and little daughter standing in the driveway I knew something was terribly wrong. Their words were heartbreaking and devastating blows despite the fact that the Judge and I had parted ways. But as my family leaned forward to give me the news I already knew that it was the Judge, that he'd been killed and it was an accident. Even with him I'd sensed something unusual and final about our last conversation. He called me just three days earlier to ask if I'd fly up for a celebration of his accomplishments in Chicago.

It was the only time I said no to the Judge. The moving van was outside my house packing for a move back to Florida. He was excited to hear I was moving to Gainesville, home of the Gators. "Get season tickets dude," was the last thing he said to me. I couldn't get him out of my mind on the long drive from Virginia to Florida and couldn't wait to get there to call him to get to arrange for him to come down for a Gator's game. There were no cell phones then. I often wonder if the Judge sensed the turn fate was making and that his death was imminent. I guess no one can ever really know these things in fact.

The Judge died on a lonely country road in Illinois. Driving blind, he'd hit an embankment at full throttle, apparently thinking that the blinking light was cautionary and not signaling a dead-end road. He'd still blown a full five years past his own determined exit date as he'd always expressed his wish to leave this mortal coil by age 30.

Did the Judge have a death wish? No! He was too full of life and I understand he was beginning to live life in a brand new way with a new purpose and drive. I always suspected his machismo spoke when he railed about "not living past thirty." It was his dude language injecting itself into the heart of an eager young leader.

I suspect that what he was really saying was he planned to live his life to the fullest, to pack it all in by age thirty so he could get on with the next phase of his life. I am proud to have lived it with him.

You are reading a story about life, laughter, tears, growth, and the God given ability to sort things out, put them into their proper slots in our mind through retrospection as we find ourselves at a crossroads as we attempt to balance the remaining ledger. It then becomes critical to understand, assert and love our true selves, I believe it's the best gift we have for the world, our most authentic self, decoded. The story is a meditation on friendship, and a tribute to one of the most significant and true friendships of my life.

Friendship

"The desire for friendship is strong in every human heart. We crave the companionship of those who understand. As the nostalgia of life compresses we sigh for 'home,' and we long for the presence of one who sympathizes with our aspirations, for one who comprehends our hopes, and is able to partake of our joys. A thought is not our own until we impart it to another, and the confessional seems to be a yearning need of every human soul. One can bear grief, but it takes two to be glad.

We reach the divine through someone, and by dividing our joy with this one we double it, and come in touch with the Universal. The sky is never so blue, the birds never sing so blithely, our acquaintances are never as gracious as when we are filled with love for someone else.

Being in harmony with one we are in harmony with all. The lover idealizes and clothes the beloved with virtues that exist only in his imagination. The beloved is consciously or unconsciously aware of this, and endeavors to fulfill the high ideal; and in the contemplation of the transcendent qualities that his mind has created, the lover is raised to heights otherwise impossible.

Should the beloved pass from this earth while such a condition of exaltation exists, the conception is indelibly impressed upon the soul, just as the last earthly view is said to be imprinted on the retina of the deceased.

The highest earthly relationship is in its very essence fleeting. Men are fallible and living in a world where the material wants jostle, time and change play their ceaseless parts, gradual obliteration comes and disillusion enters. But the memory of a sweet affinity once fully possessed and snapped by fate at its most supreme moment, can never die from our heart.

All other troubles are swallowed up in this; and if the individual is of too stern a fiber to be completely crushed into the dust, time will come bearing healing, and the memory of that once ideal condition will chant in his heart a perpetual Eucharist.

I hope the world has passed forever from the nightmare of pity for the dead; they have ceased from their labors and are at rest. But for the living, when death has entered and removed the best friend, fate has done her worst; the plummet has sounded the depths of grief, and thereafter nothing can inspire terror.

At one fell stroke all petty annoyances and corroding cares are sunk into nothingness. The memory of a great friendship lives enshrined in undying amber. It affords ballast against all the storms that blow, and although it lends an unutterable sadness, it imparts an unspeakable peace. Where there is this haunting memory of a great friend lost, there is also forgiveness, charity, and sympathy that make the man brother to all who suffer and endure.

The individual himself is nothing; he has nothing to hope for, nothing to lose, nothing to win, and this constant memory of the high and exalted friendship that was once his is a nourishing source of strength; it constantly purifies the mind and inspires the heart to nobler living and diviner thinking. The man is in communication with elemental conditions.

To have known an ideal friendship, and have it fade from your grasp and flee as a shadow before it is touched with the sordid breath of selfishness, or sullied by misunderstanding, is the highest good. And the constant dwelling in sweet, sad recollection of the exalted virtues of the one that is gone tends to crystallize these very virtues in the heart of he who mediates upon them." These truly inspiring words by Elbert Hubbard were written in 1912. Doc and the Judge believe this all to be true.

Thanks for joining me on this voyage back. I've been documenting this period for several years; the intention was to pay homage to a friend and to document an incredible and unimpeachable friendship. Along the way, as with life itself, as I drifted back to my own childhood in search of self; I also found focus on defining moments that shaped my course, they became an intrinsic subtext to my simple sentimental journey.

This self sought sabbatical has offered me the first opportunity in my life for an extended freedom from the demands, challenges and yes the rewards of a career, to entirely deconstruct my habitual life. I gave myself entirely and greedily to the process. I relished the surprises and the frustrations I endured and along the way I discovered my own priceless treasure trove of memories submerged over many years by the accumulating and suffocating daily dross.

Finding my memories percolating to the surface of my consciousness was as gratifying and life changing as discovering and making the acquaintance of a brother or sister you never knew. The connection dazzled my olfactory center where references as primal as smell, sound and a collective cornucopia of moments of my life found me then proceeded to overwhelm me.

The unadulterated joy of these cascading memories discovered drove me onward to explore further, to seek out more and more with a drive I suspect rivaled that of an addict looking for their next score. This has been the most fulfilling, the most fortifying and certainly the most grounding project of my life. The privilege was all mine and now I humbly share it with you.

It's such a gift to be able to sit, walk, or even think. Oh my, the luxury to think is such an underrated and under explored blessing. I quote Socrates on this point who often and pleadingly implored that, "The unexplored life was not worth the living."

The thrill of a full life without being plugged in like some alien android to pulsating, vibrating and beeping Blackberry's and cell phones is beyond my ability to express. I have had the luxury to read, enjoy the landscape, travel, get reacquainted with my God by studying scriptures underlined by my elders in an old family bible and passed on to me by my mother, and above all strengthen my spirit and along the way document my soul's most ardent whispers.

I now understand more fully my life's path. I understand that my enduring relationship with my mother, how precious it was, how its essence guides and sustains me still. I recognize today that this bond was based on faith, give and take, mutual love and respect. I understand that the brat in me was overstated; somehow I just knew how to get what I wanted, which essentially was guided by the hard-work principle that I learned by example from an early age.

I understand that my father didn't know how to express emotions and was particularly clumsy like men of his generation with affection; however, he left me a legacy of strength, common sense, hard work, good values, pride in accomplishment and an abiding love for family.

I suspect some of those friends in the tent from that night many decades ago may still be grappling with the erection issue. I know that my love for soul, country, and rock music of my day are inherently a core love. I know in unique ways I receive wisdom from every member of my family, I know too that every experience I've had with friends and associates has bought out the best in us both.

I know the Jazzman was my alternate father figure. I know that the Judge was a great friend, as close as a brother and he's forever a part of me. I know that I had more fun in the 70's than any "code" should permit. I don't believe I'm special; indeed I've done nothing extraordinary that would qualify as having contributed a great deal to the "amelioration of mankind." However, I'm recognizing I've come full circle in my life. I feel blessed and I feel very, very good, and I knew that I would, just like the iconic Godfather of Soul, James Brown always promised!

I'm most happy when people whose paths I've crossed in business or life say that a word or thought I shared had positive influence and meaning for their lives. Many I've known have conquered a great deal themselves and they're confident in their contributions. They've had their own impressive successes both personally and professionally.

I'm most saddened however, when I talk to people of my generation whose lives are complicated, some fighting alcoholism or drugs while some grapple a fundamental search for self-worth. These people still seek reconciliation as they desperately search for understanding in their lives. They recognize that all too quickly the sands of the hour glass sink toward the bottom with whatever time remains being precious. They sadly recognize what time does remain is very fragile, finite and sacred.

I know we share the same questions, the same thoughts and concerns about who we believe we are, where we've been, where we're going, and the ever present question of how much time in fact remains for each of us to work out life's remaining questions that presently remain unresolved.

We are not the first and won't be the last to face such challenging existential questions. Life gives us ample opportunity to resolve all questions that remain for each of us. Life is fluid; it ebbs and flows until the very end, it's up to each of us to choose wisely at least at the most prescient periods of stability and introspection of those lives with what time remains.

I've seen people at various stages of life experience an awakening when the light suddenly goes on and a sense of purpose permeates. I've experienced people in their last hours and moments of life coming to resolution in their lives and communion with their soul's maker then pass on with a sense of peace and grace having given it all up in the end to the keeper of the highest order of life. They finally gave in with a sense of relief and resignation thus purging their minds of perceived wrongdoings, exonerating their immortal self thereby leaving this life as it began, serene, pure, expectant, ready to embrace the next chapter that we all reverentially seek in the hereafter.

I feel very fortunate that my own "light of resolution" went on early enough to allow me adequate time to sort through my personal matters. I love my life today, I reverence my God and my close union with him and thank him often in great gratitude for all who are in it. I am blessed. I hope you feel you have many blessings too. I hope you have angels in your life for whose gracious companionship in your life you gladly thank and praise God.

It only remains now for me to thank you for giving me this opportunity to share my thoughts. As you've read along, I hope you agree that there are no secrets between us. If I've motivated one person to slow down, pan the vista that is their life at large, take in the sumptuous natural world that surrounds them I will be pleased indeed.

If I can coax some to pull back the layers and go from the macro external world to the micro world of introspection I ask that you trust in self to explore your deepest, truest self to pull your essential spirit back to the surface. If this happens then I will have far exceeded my most deep and ardent ambition. I ask you to explore, I ask you to forgive and learn to love, accept and even enjoy yourself again.

It never fails to surprise me how people can be found professing their love of spouse, children, country, food types, pets and favorite colors and so on. I believe we are all compassionate, loving and forgiving in the image of our God. I yearn to have a time when we can as easily profess this compassion, love and forgiveness for our long suffering selves.

We live in complex duality, we must coexist with the best of who we are and the reality of the self who only learns, grows, and experiences in meaningful ways through error and realignment based on hard earned and hard learned gritty life experiences. We will have come a long way in terms of self-actualization and we will have gone a long way to winning the long raging battle against self-loathing that permeates many societies.

God has never punished us, why must we continue in nil sum gain relationships with others who seek to destroy us. Walk away in the knowledge that you learned valuable lessons about seeking the most discriminating relationships which enhance your own God spirit. Not every soul is meant to live in close quarters with every other soul, this is why we pull the best of others toward us that fit and enhance our truest self.

Finally if you will not suffer spiritual battery from another ask yourself in your darkest truest moments how you could allow yourself to torment, punish and crush your spirit day after grueling day. This existential experience of ours is a "walk on, give it all you have" proposition. We recoil in rage and empathy at the sight of abuse of dog, child, worker in the workforce and so on. Ask yourself then how and more importantly why we would deign to counter intuitively persist in self-loathing, self-hatred and self-abuse that loops through our heads, through our hearts, manifests in alcoholism, drug abuse, eating disorders, this truth is at the root of our self-destruction and is antithetical to everything God desires for every one of us.

I long to awake to the day we may love self, respect self, long to explore, nurture and grow self back to our God's image of the greatness that he reverentially endowed each and every one of us with. I wish to be present for the day we all truthfully and forcibly profess our abiding sense of love for self which is on par with the love we feel for the world and all its dazzling and majestic favors and diversions. I'll feel that I have made a modest contribution to my universal family. I always seek to do "good," it's in my DNA but in truth I also seek to do good with an eye to my mother's good opinion. She was and remains my personal high water mark for goodness, she was goodness personified and I seek to continue to earn her pride and faith and keep them residing in me.

Stay with me just a little longer as we make our Pacific crossing.

The Judge's Been Gone for a Quarter of a Century

The Judge and I loved Australia, and he knew I would never travel there without him and nor would he travel there without me for that matter. Our love for Australia began with conversations with a friend and world class surfer Gary Propper. Gary put Australian surfing right up there with Hawaii and California, in particular he talked about surfing in Queensland, at Bondi Beach in Sydney, and Geelong. We had to go there. The love for Australia grew as we met and talked with members of AC/DC, the Little River Band, and a great band, Cold Chisel, when they toured America with Cheap Trick and Ted Nugent. The commitment to travel to Australia was sealed after we finished the Florida leg of Billy Thorpe's *Children of the Sun* tour. Every show sold out and the Miami stop had people lined up around the block waiting to buy tickets just in case Billy decided to do a third show. The Judge wanted to welcome Billy to America in style. He promised to welcome Billy on the radio with the same royal treatment other super stars received, after all Billy Thorpe was a super "super star" in Australia but only remained to be discovered in America.

The Judge welcomed Billy by playing the album *Children of the Sun* fifty times on the radio in the weeks leading up to the scheduled show. The Judge started with cut 1 then tracked it all the way through alternating music with a veritable travelogue on the beauty of Australia about which he then knew little. He always told me he'd wanted to see Australia and to this end he sought all sorts of information with a voracity that was disarming and charming.

First there was business to be done, along the way though we became fast and fervent friends with Billy and this sealed the deal on our firming plans "down under" bound. We all twittered excitedly about the reunion and fun we'd have in Australia. Sadly the plans took a backseat to real life and the promise of the trip was always answered with a "soon dude." Nevertheless the prospect of the gathering plan delighted the Judge.

We promised to visit Billy assuring him of our need to beat the countdown to the Judge's 30th birthday which by now even Billy recognized the significance of having experienced the Judge's frenetic lifestyle first hand. Sadly the right opportunity never presented during the Judge's brief life. I now find myself tracking down our pal Billy in anticipation to fulfill that long promised trip we'd all spoken of those many years earlier.

Fate dealt another unexpected hand as sadly shortly thereafter I got word Billy had died. In all honesty it never felt entirely right to make plans to catch up with Billy after all these years, not without the Judge.

My wife is Australian and has spent many holidays in the northern coastal region of New South Wales. She felt sure the local color and character of the area would help recapture the spirit of those remarkable days when Doc, the Judge and Billy the Kid were inseparable and reigned supreme. She knew I was in a funk about Billy's death and felt this environment would stir my writing juices.

Nimbin, she explained is an alternative lifestyle "mecca" in Australia, adding if any place could help capture the vibe of Billy's spirit it would be here. I instinctively knew the Judge would find and meet me there among the hippies and flower children. The Judge never missed a great party or a radical new trip. I instantly sensed his presence.

The Judge is always present at parties, any place in fact where imbibing is likely. I suspect every tipple and toast enjoyed is interpreted by him as another salute to his fabulous memory. In our hay day whenever there was a party it was understood that whoever else may be in attendance the Judge alone held the honor of "imbiber in chief" and "party animal in chief." In short, the party was wherever the Judge was.

Even when it seems the Judge isn't nearby, he manages to send some cosmic wink confirming his presence. This is done with a spontaneous explosion of a shot glass as someone orders a Wild Turkey. Of a more personal nature a feel-up of the tightest bottoms at a gathering is not at all uncommon.

He always fancied himself the contemporary lady killer rivaled as I've said earlier only by Mozart's infamous lothario Don Giovanni. I'm not sure how the metaphysical world works but I'm not surprised the Judge has found his own unique and direct way to communicate his presence. On some occasions his delivery system is very grand and theatrical indeed! No matter.

We left Sydney for the 8 hour drive up to Nimbin along the Pacific Highway and planned to swing through Byron Bay for a few days of rollicking in the magnificent turquoise beaches of this lovely town. It famously is the easterly most point in Australia and girded majestically by the Pacific Ocean up and down its length.

We left Sydney weaving through heavy traffic working our way along the Pacific Highway on an unseasonably dull day now pouring with rain. We knew Australia's been in severe drought for many years, that the water catchment area is depleted by 50% of normal capacity. This rain's steady, inconvenient, but much needed.

The farther north we get on our sojourn the more the rain intensifies. Then heavens literally open and we're deluged. We hear from locals that there's a cyclone, Cyclone Helen (the southern hemispheres name for a hurricane) in Northern Queensland and we're told we've caught the nasty back end of her as she brings on torrential downpours, flash flooding and mud slides.

By now our backs ache and our heads throb with the relentless and amplified thump of the rain all around the car battering it. Not long from our destination now and rain begins to pound so hard the VW Golf shakes and dangerously begins to slide on the road. We pull over at McDonalds to see the worst out safely.

Traffic almost clears off all roads as both vision and safety are utterly impossible. Travelers offer harrowing accounts describing it as the worst tempest in decades, others report services are out, bridges are closed and statewide evacuation in progress in some areas as Cyclone Helen pummels north east Australia.

Rain bands strike our northern New South Wales destination relentlessly and hard and low lying regions are quickly flooded, many submerged under depths of sitting water. The Judge is smiling somewhere recognizing the ironic perfection of our arrival in Florida style hurricane and its devastation.

The Judge and I had endured many hurricanes together over the years on the "event prone" Atlantic coast. He'd be screaming rock 'n' roll and urging us to press on full steam … in the old days. And if he'd been there in the Golf with us that night he'd have urged us onward then too. "Crash or crash through dude," was a memorable quote of the Judge's.

So as the worst of the storm eases we head out again, after a couple of hours and nearing our destination even our intrepid souls recognize we need to stop if we mean to survive this ordeal. And so as our survival instinct kicks in we seek out a place to bunk down from the wild weather, we plan to celebrate our delayed honeymoon alive rather than risking celebrating it in hospital.

Every hotel, motel, and manger was occupied – shit, we were stuck! We spotted a lonely caravan park (RV Park) off a lovely swelling river just turning its lights off for the night as we approach it. We drive in and talk our way into a wee box, in fact the home of the grounds keeper who's currently away, the lucky bastard!

We pay a king's ransom for a box by the flooding river. We've done the deal and are relieved to get off the treacherous road in these wild conditions. Who knows if the sudden change in weather from sunshine and broken clouds to cyclonic gale force winds was the Judge's doing but we keep vigil expecting new surprises and further signs.

We shower and change but we're exhausted so we have a nightcap and go to sleep, we don't even check the TV for weather updates or news. Miraculously, the next morning we're back to brilliant sunshine and we drive our final miles to Nimbin. As we reach Casino, the major town just out of Nimbin, we find last night's deluge has flooded every road to Nimbin. Police on the scene of a roadblock tell us it's the worst flooding in the area since 1951. Huh, the very year the Judge is born. I'm no expert but I'd say this was another wink from the Judge who's never understated.

We watch for more signs as we weave through dazzling glorious, lush endless green pastures dotted with emerald trees. This sumptuous landscape is complete with what I think to be incredible volcanic boulders the like of which I've seldom seen. These then are perfectly placed by a heavenly hand in proportion and positioned to frame the perfection of the mountains rising against the endless sky.

"This surely is God's own country," you know the old cliché. In truth and notwithstanding there are no words to truly do the vision justice; this quite breathtaking, spectacular vista overwhelms you from every angle.

A local we stop to ask for directions draws a makeshift road map to help us navigate the flooded roads. It's a horse trail more than a road in fact he advises, and it's apparently the way this horseman always got around flooding in the past but today even this road is a river. We spot Nimbin on the other side of the hill a few kilometers away but there's a caravan of cars dead ended there by the lapping water of the rising surge.

We heard locals murmuring, "I was born and raised here and can't remember the last time this road flooded." Others lamented, "See that house on the hill there mate, well before building they asked about the possibility of flooding being a problem in the area, and they were told what, flooding here? No never, absolutely no flooding worries here mate and look at this road now!" Look at it would you… it looks like a whole lot of flooding to me," he quipped.

We met one lovely young couple with three adorable little children all on their way back home from a wedding in Brisbane and they were stranded here too and just meters from their home which they too could see but could not reach. The young wife said she bred alpacas and they'd be frightened and hungry by now, she was desperate to get home to tend to them.

We talked to land owners, mostly small operators in horse and cattle who knew from generations past that this road never flooded, and incredibly reported that even as little as an hour ago it wasn't flooded. I faced northeast towards the Judge in Florida to ask, "Dude, how'd you do this?" The message echoed back that there was a surprise in store for us in Nimbin where an important player would seek us out.

We had just arrived for a pit stop when a young man whose name I would soon learn was Phillip Peterkin approached me with the directness of an arranged rendezvous. He boldly walked toward me, held out a firm hand, slaps my back then says, "I can tell you're a groover." Meanwhile my wife stepped into a shop to buy us each a drink while I prefer to wait outside and enjoy the street scene.

This young man tells me he's a painter who'd set out for an annual art festival on a local river island but was washed out of his jeep which was dragged off the road in the flash floods. He'd lost his jeep and sustained water damage to most of his paintings. I recognized Phillip as the player the Judge advised would, "seek you out dude."

Phillip walked with authority in his gait toward me with a stack of his salvaged paintings under his other arm. He says he's waiting for his mother to pick him up. Most of the art work he had hoped to sell was water damaged. He sensed my interest in seeing his work and without solicitation he scurried to a magnificent sandstone façade of the local Catholic Church, returning quickly with more of his paintings.

He laid out fourteen original paintings and walked us through his thoughts and intentions for each piece. He eagerly sought our impression of each one listening intently to our thoughts. Each piece required close inspection as he layered his symbolism with bold new concepts emerging from every glance. He asked what we felt they might be worth; we told him honestly we felt they were all priceless. He lamented that they'd all need cleaning and then refinishing but we urged him to leave the slight discoloration as it was now part of the provenance of the paintings.

We told him they were all beautiful, and we'd love to buy a piece from him but we had no money as the ATM machines were down the last days from the cyclone. "No, you don't understand, this isn't about money," he urged "I'm here for you to pick out your painting."

Peterkin's painting not surprisingly called "Judgment" spoke powerfully to us when he described his emergence from drug use. Again he urged us to accept it with his best wishes to us for a great honeymoon and working holiday. Special encounters like this are reminders that very little in life is coincidental. The Judge surely had a hand in this chance meeting just as he'd predicted in the days before.

We engaged in a quiet, spiritual discussion with this young artist, we'd broached all manner of subjects from existentialism, the merits of the *Celestine Prophecy* right through to great cuisine and everything in between. He apologized for the dalliance into food but said he was getting hungry. We had some incredible spinach and ricotta pastries that my wife had grabbed to snack on for the road trip. We asked that he have them to tide him over until his mother arrived. He'd too had had his own formative and epic journey during this time.

A few days in Nimbin feels like a few days in Key West. The alternative life style is deeply rooted. The headline in the local paper was dedicated to the passing of Chicken George who's something of a local hero and who'd recently died of throat cancer. He was a quintessential Australian larrikin who'd been everywhere, done everything and in his dotage had chosen Nimbin and all it represents to live out his final years in reverence for life and in personal authenticity.

By all accounts he was a great story teller, a tribal leader to the younger locals. We sensed both how deeply he was loved and how fully his loss was felt by the eulogizing we heard of Chicken George all around town among the locals.

His mantle was being passed to Michael who seems equally qualified to keep order and balance in this delightful haven. Indeed, as we prepared to leave town to press on with our trip we watched Michael break up a fight between two exuberant youths in front of the Nimbin Museum. This unique gallery houses a collection among other things of fronts, sides, and backs of authentic old VW bugs adorned with signs of peace, love and anti-war emblems. The next collection was of a myriad of bongs – all operational and regularly being used I'm quite sure. The Judge chortled heartily at this sight. I imagined I'd heard him whisper his ubiquitous, "Rock 'n' roll dude."

The spirit of Nimbin seems to come down to an awareness of order, opportunity and a compelling desire to live free, unfettered and authentic lives. In this spirit many services provided are free including the bus service and the local paper among other things. Restaurant offerings in Nimbin cover the gambit ranging from gourmet Asian influenced food, vegetarian, vegan and smoothie houses. No mention of food is complete in Australia without the ever present and ever popular fish and chips shops. Naturally fast food junkies were also catered to including hamburgers, tacos, pastries and delicious fresh local produce.

Yes, it reminds me of Key West. The alternative scene there however is predominantly a gay scene of resplendent, defiant young boys and young girls strolling hand in hand. It always seemed to me that their displays were motivated mostly to be a declaration of sexual freedom rather than an expression of personal freedom per se.

In Nimbin it appears the objective is to live in peace with authenticity. I feel at home here, a deep bond grows in me for Nimbin, its people and its philosophy. Moreover, I'm confident the Judge would have wanted to get close to Nimbin too.

My favorite Australian bumper sticker spotted in Nimbin: "I lost my virginity but still have the box it came in." Right on!

Australia

We travelled to Australia leaving a dusting of snow over the hut in my beloved Sonora and arrived in Sydney in the beginning of their long hot summer which we found out this year was not to be so hot. In fact we arrived on the first day of the New Year. This summer we found locals saying everywhere that this was a summer like no other they'd experienced.

We were welcomed with wild weather fluctuations including drought, cyclone and flood. Cold one morning and hot the next and vice versa. Sunshine also alternated with heavy rain clouds day after day so there was very little predictability as to what the next hour might bring.

I was at home with the birdlife which is lush, loud and oh the glorious colors of the birds teeming and abundant even in the suburbs. Birds begin the day in waves of bird symphonies beginning with the black sorrows (crows) which will lead in with the crowing at sunrise. This invariably wakes the entire bird population from near and far. Kookaburras cackle and this is colloquially referred to as singing or laughing. The elegant black and white Kurrawongs screech in their own fashion then there's the sulphur crested Cockatoos, pink Galahs and assorted Lorikeets, Parakeets, Cockies and Parrots, Budgerigars and Rosellas and countless others beauties.

They all belong to the parrot family and they thrive, cackle, perch and chatter all day long. I came to think of this cacophony of sounds throughout the day as their unique version of the famous bush telegraph. Budgies and finch abound in this bird idyll and respond to the world and their imperatives in their own way.

Before too long a crescendo of thousands of assorted birds fluttering and chirping in symphonic unison among the eucalyptus trees ensues – dawn is a magical time here. The tooting sound of the commuter train urgently chugging onto its next station reinforces the fact that everyone is waking, preparing for the new day and getting on trains to their offices downtown in

Sydney's central business district.

Sydney is a big successful rail city. Otherwise the drive-time traffic jams in this city of around 5 million would fall into total grid lock. Instead, this rail experience is a quite seamless and gentile journey moving everyone everywhere or at least part of the way toward their final destination. There's a terrific feeling of freedom on the streets and in the airports that I've not felt in 25 years in America. I hope to find this feeling is never lost here.

The Judge would have stood tall in Australia. I know now people come to Australia to live, not to die. The Judge would have loved what he'd have found here, seen, heard and above all he'd have loved all that Australia stands for. Australia is young, edgy, smart and fast. Sydney is the youngest, edgiest and fastest city in Australia without a doubt. Australia has forged strong family, business and political ties with America. American news is prominent throughout the day in telecast and broadcast reports and like most countries Australia looks to America as a business, political and social barometer for new trends.

The adage here is, "If America sneezes then Australia will surely catch cold," which lends testimony to the ties that bind our nations. Australia's vast investment in America ensures they enjoy our good times and conversely suffer our bad along with us. Unfortunately this is the reality of business contagion theory in the global economy we now live in. I sensed Australia's youth in particular currently blames America for the current economic difficulties.

We were fortunate to be in Australia's capital city Canberra on the 12th and 13th of February as Australia's new Prime Minister Kevin Rudd who just weeks into his electoral win stood before Parliament and called a symbolic "sorry day" for the Stolen Generation of Aboriginal children.

The vast and breathtaking grounds of the Parliamentary precinct in Canberra, buttressed between the dazzling new Parliament House and the now retired but distinguished old Parliament House, housed tens of thousands of indigenous leaders, citizens and thousands of Anglo Saxon supporters recognizing this historic event. They sat on the lawn under makeshift cover in the torrential rain to bear witness to the utterance of the words they and their ancestors hoped to one day hear while secretly fearing they may never.

It was incredibly moving and very much like the period of civil agitation around the memorials in Washington DC's White House precinct. We all remember the impact and power of those politically charged gatherings outside the White House during the restless 60's.

Here in Canberra inside the Parliamentary building the Prime Minister's speech to the nation was preceded by an elaborate Aboriginal ritual of "official welcome to country." In light of circumstances and history, it was a very generous offer of welcome to the country at that. I noticed it put some less hardy dignitaries to sleep while others tapped busy feet to the mesmerizing rhythm of the didgeridoo.

The majority however betrayed beaming smiles overwhelmed with pride at how far the nation had come in race relations. Eyes welled with tears, a sudden spontaneous burst of thousands of voices erupted into chants. Emotional words of sorrow and respect were spoken and heartfelt offerings of apology were spoken from the Prime Minister and the Leader of the Opposition. It was a unique moment as genuine acceptance of each for the other was made possible. It was broadcast around the world offering hope to all people and nations.

This indeed was a national watershed day for race relations in Australia. It was a day that touched the nation's soul and poignantly began an overdue process of healing. This ceremonial sorry day was a national apology for the sadly misguided policy of removing half cast children from Aboriginal families.

This policy long blighted the nation and its citizens of good will. The stolen generation were Aboriginal children removed from violence within families mostly borne upon mixed blood children who were treated harshly in their own community as half cast and not "Aboriginal" enough.

This is the perennial plight of half cast children around the world in particularly difficult moments in history. They remained a stark reminder of social dislocation, they looked different, didn't fit in comfortably and were an unsettling reminder of the Aboriginal resentment of the usurpation of their homeland.

Though the children bore the brunt of racism consistent with the times, they bore no knowledge or fault in the events as they played out socially. Sadly they bore only the scars of its consequential persecution through the years.

The children were put into orphanages or adopted into white families who wanted to give them safe and loving environments. The heartbreak of breaking up families without consent lingers on; the pain lingers like a malignancy, passes from generation to generation erupting from time to time into social upheaval against this tragic policy and its unforgivable legacy.

Such was Sorry Day. Old hurt, new hurt, injustice and prejudice, survivors, and victims all gathered all welcomed here on this magnificent, moving day. First and second generation survivors spoke eloquently about the meaning of this symbolic day and for the nation to reflect upon. Legislators solemnly promised before God, in the sacred halls of Australia's National Parliament Building and before the nation that never again may this be allowed to happen again. Sorry.

Movingly, the tens of thousands of Australia's Aboriginals assembled watching the service broadcast on giant TV monitors and they all wore T-shirts made for the day emblazoned simply with the words "thank you" against the backdrop of thousands of waving Aboriginal flags which symbolize red for earth, yellow for sun and a large black circle in the center of the these 2 block color horizons symbolizing the Aboriginal people themselves, marking their place at the very nexus of sun and earth in their homeland of Australia.

Sorry is beautiful.

Sorry is powerful.

Nearing the End

What happens in life is we slowly become more like we were meant to be. It's a painstaking process to peel back the layers to find our way back to the beginning to find those deeply seeded precious gems defining who and what we are. A loved one will know the questions to ask to help you find your way. Once there, it is an equally painstaking process to bring forth the real you and work it into its rightful place and prominence. As my mother lay dying, she had parting words for her three sons. To me, she said, "You were always the best at everything you did, and you did so with little effort. You always celebrated others' accomplishments. You are working too hard. Success will always be yours but money isn't everything. Find your way back to the person I know you are. I love you and I will find you in heaven."

There are two kinds of knowledge. That which is stored away as fact gained from years of training and experience, the other knowing where to go to research the missing information. The Internet today gives us the freedom to travel anywhere to receive whatever information we seek, this is as revolutionary as the horseless carriage allowing us to leave familiar surroundings in search of recreation, exploration, fellowship, and commerce.

But the real information we yearn to know and relentlessly seek is information about ourselves, this is found only within, by going straight to the core. Our parents, grandparents, and great grandparents were the elders of our culture. They're an added source of information in our quest to make sense of our place in the world we inhabit, in short who we are and how to better serve ourselves, our communities and our maker, with the time we've been given.

If you're a collector, surround yourself with pictures of your past. If a writer, then write about your culture. If you're a thinker construct opportunities and creative portals for cultural co-existence while boldly affirming our American culture and heritage. If you're a dreamer, look and work toward better tomorrow's, work toward self-sufficiency, work toward inspiring aspiration in all citizens. Work toward a day when all may equally hope to improve their lot in life, as you pray silently and fervently that they find the requisite motivation to attain all they need.

Engage your passion and work tirelessly for superior education for all children and for affordable health care for all citizens. Seek a world of good triumphing over despair and a world where attorneys are held to the highest ethical standard. Demand our policy makers spend all their time and energy devoted to the service of their constituents and ask them that they too live up to their preaching.

The effect of goodness is powerful and contagious. Its presence in our lives leads to more positive change and a momentum toward more good things just around the corner. Don't allow men who spend all their time in private jets scold you to cycle more and excoriate you about your carbon footprint. Defy them to lead by example and themselves live up to their preaching.

Good deeds grow in every heart, goodness permeates every middle class home, generosity and the spirit of public service is alive and triumphant in America's middle class. Let others reveal their own endeavors to serve nation, neighbor and God. The middle class no longer waits for the rest of the nation to act, instead the middle class defiantly leads the charge in charity specific needs such as Katrina and Ike in America or Indonesia's horrific tsunami over the Christmas season in 2004/2005. In general terms too it's the great middle class who is never too busy to donate its time, money, and to lend its support to others less fortunate.

It's not charity of the heart and soul to attend a multi thousands of dollars per head event as you claim the evening against your taxes a charitable donation. You have done nothing in any way to heal your soul, serve your God or in any meaningful fashion help another human being either in fact or in principal. If it's doesn't feel like an act of charity given with heart and humility it's probably style trumping substance and selling itself as something it clearly is not.

To be useful, you must continue to grow. To have a servant's heart and a charitable soul you must be offering of yourself to another in their hour of need. An honest exchange of humility i.e. a humble offering of self with the silent prayer "that there but for the grace of God go I" and in exchange the receipt with humility, grace and gratitude of that charitable offering is the essential equation of charity at work in a human exchange. A sage man once said wisely, "When you stop growing you start dying." When we stop "giving," our lives, souls and hearts become no more than commodities for the marketplace.

Doc and the Judge

Welcome Back

Welcome back my friends to a journey that never ends. I've been waiting here for you as you've read on. I've been thinking about who you are, where in life you find yourself and I've wondered above all what you'll say when we meet.

The season is turning here in Sonora. Last night I looked straight up into the black sky as it spread about me encrusted with infinite dazzling stars. My eyes swept across and caught sight of the full moon as she lay perfectly suspended, shining heavy, golden and pregnant on the horizon emblazoned with seven brilliant stars sparkling incandescent like diamond jewels around her as if to signify her prominence and provenance.

The mystery and majesty of the moment last night for me harkened back to the fateful evening for the three magi on their date with destiny over 2009 years earlier. If you are very still and very quiet you'll hear the message on the wind whispering of a new cycle, softly affirming that there's always new hope just around the corner if you will just believe.

Naturally, the Judge has the final word. "Hey dude I read our book and it shits!" he chortles in his inimitable way then adds, "Clever, though, and I'm feeling groovy." With a final flourish he ends thus, "Now you see what happens when I leave you alone, you go drifting off into all that psychosocial babble."

"What the fuck's wrong with you dude? Relax, grab a 'girl' and get yourself a boat or something!" He paused for effect then nailed me with, "And hey, did you ever correct that wicked slice? Have you fulfilled your dream of playing in the Pro-Am at Pebble?"

Always the name dropper he added, "As for me, Doc, I tee off at two with guess who? A hint, dude, he drives a forty-year-old Rolls Royce golf cart and still finds every water hazard. I know I'll see you again soon, you straight, fucked up, smart ass, Georgia farm boy." Finally, as he left for his date with

Jackie Gleason he finished with, "Oh yeah, Jazzman and the Sportscaster still hold court with the old farts during cocktail hour. Damn I wish you'd bring them some new stories!"

Till then … She's only rock 'n' roll, bitch!

Doc and the Judge!

About the Author

Born and raised in Thomaston, Ga., Gary (Doc) Granger's lifelong profession as a broadcaster began at age 15 as a disc jockey at WQXI, Atlanta. His life has afforded him a dizzying array of experiences and opportunities with memorable highs including sharing the stage with the Beatles in Atlanta, decades of peerless service to the broadcasting industry, a 'jarhead' with the USMCR during the Viet Nam era and the thrill of a deep abiding, lifelong friendship with the Judge who was the quintessential American original. Gary writes about a decade of many memorable experiences shared with his friend the Judge during the Rock 'n' Roll 70's. He and the Judge had a pact that if one of them survived the 70's he would write about those experiences. Doc survived to fulfill the promise made to his friend, and in doing so discovers himself all over again…

Gary seeks to understand the soft vulnerable underbelly of humanity. He seeks to understand himself and has maintained a lifelong interest in and fascination with the collective "us:" the sibling, stranger, colleague, nurse, teacher, firefighter, policemen and women, foot soldier, the prodigious child and the social pariah equally. The kings among us and the pawns are of equal value as souls and therefore of equal interest to this modern anthropologist as he clinically dissecting what it means to be human.

Those who know Gary Granger have heard him urgently ask "when is the war won?" Herein lays the secret code to understanding this complex man. He champions every individual who acts with honor, valor courage and integrity. He stands against corruption, discrimination and has championed those who have no voice.

He enjoyed a warm friendship with Martin Luther King though he was many years MLK's junior. He is the Swiss watch maker extraordinaire who pulls his next masterpiece apart for the simple pleasure of seeing its precision internals at work. He admires the exquisite beauty and perfection of the instrument as he carefully studies and assesses any failings or flaws.

His lifelong passion has been an abiding curiosity regarding the question of what it is to be human. Music has always been his muse: country, rock, and soul. A close friendship with Charlie Daniels speaks of his first love of country music forged in Georgia in his grandmother's home as they absorbed country music singing along out loud to every song the radio played. He's the study of a modern man who's ecumenical 'music church' makes room for all great music. He acknowledges the people who conceived it, wrote it, played it and recorded it. Between these pages you'll find the inside scoop on unbelievable and unforgettable stories of the day of two dudes who were there when FM radio was coming into prominence.

Acknowledgment

I'd like to give sincere thanks and gratitude to individuals without whose assistance and input this book might not have come about as perfectly as it did.

I offer deep gratitude to my wife and daughter for their helpful edits and reedits along this voyage. I heartily thank my publisher Warren Croyle at Reality Press for his fulsome support and enthusiastic dedication to the integrity of the work. Next, I'd like to thank Laura Croyle who gave the words her imprimatur.

I'd like to thank Randolph Holder for many kindnesses over many years including the care he showed my wife and me during her battle with terminal breast cancer.

I'd like to encourage you to visit docandthejudge.com. I also take this opportunity to thank Kraig Sederquist at Clarke Broadcasting-Web Development in Sonora, CA for the dazzling work he and his staff created on the site for you my dear reader.

I'd like to send a thank you to Senior Police Constable Ian Reeney from Launceston Tasmania, Australia for the memorable police escort he gave my wife and me. We disembarked our ship in Davenport Harbor picked up our car then set off on the drive to Launceston where we would hunker down for an extended stay. It was very late, we were weary, and I was still adjusting to driving on the "wrong" side of the road. Constable Reeney got us to our destination safely with police escort. It's where the writing of this book continued and the start of a true love affair for us with Tasmania in general and Launceston in particular who's natural, rugged beauty and special people inspired me to complete this triumphant tour de force; *Doc and the Judge.*

Visit www.docandthejudge.com.

Reality is what you make it

RE REALITY PRESS

LIFE CHANGING BOOKS AND DVDS BY REALITY PRESS

Tranceformers, Shamans of the 21st century
by Dr. John. J. Harper
foreward by Dr. Bruce Lipton
362 pages, $19.95 USD
isbn 0-9777904-0-1

The true story of this author's contact with a deceased physicist colleague that forced him to confront spiritual dilemmas we all face: Who are we? Why are we here? Where are we going? After 10 years of extensive research, the author derived that Trance—the method employed by the shaman is the doorway to the fifth dimensional field of cosmic consciousness.

Montauk Babies
(the many lives of Al Leedskalnin)
(the many lives of Al Leedskalnin)
by O.H. Krill
edited and illustrated by John Malloy
111 pages, 17.95 USD
isbn 0-9777904-2-8

"The past, present and future will merge into a finite point and no-one, I mean NO-ONE knows what the outcome will be, we must prepare the people for the coming change". Al Leedskalnin tells it like it is just days prior to the year 2012. While scientist Peabody Freeman and Al are on 'accident duty', the world outside has no idea that the end is near.

STEIGERWERKS CLASSICS SERIES!

Revelation, The Divine Fire
by Brad Steiger
258 pages, 19.95 USD
isbn 09777904-7-9

A Biblical prediction says "In the latter days, your sons and daughters shall prophesy." Brad Steiger has communicated with literally hundreds of individuals who claim to have received messages directly from God, or from spacemen, angels, spirit guides, or other superhuman entities and has documented these experiences in this SteigerWerks Classic. Revelation, The Divine Fire rings more profound and true than when first published in 1973.

Secrets of the Serpent, In Search of the Sacred Past
by Philip Gardiner
156 pages, 17.95 USD
isbn 0-9777904-3-6

Philip Gardiner reveals the world's most mysterious places were once sacred to the Serpent Cult. The history and mythology of the so-called reptilian agenda and alien visitation in ancient times now has a solid opponent. In this book the author reveals the real "bloodline" spoken of by Dan Brown in the Da Vinci Code.

Your Immortal Body of Light
by Mitchell Earl Gibson, M.D.
126 pages, 17.95 USD
isbn 0-9777904-5-2

Dr. Gibson was Chief Resident in Psychiatry at a large inner city medical center when he began his journey, expanding his consciousness using meditation. On his quest, he actually encounters an ancient 'god of healing' known as Djehuti (pronounced Dee-jan-tee), or Thoth. Both fascinating and chilling this is not your everyday spiritual awakening story.

**All Online Orders receive a
FREE Reality Entertainment CD sampler
to order go to
www.reality-entertainment.com/books.htm**

toll free order desk 1-866-585-1355

for wholesale inquries contact info@reality-entertainment.com

coming soon Reality Audio Books
featuring the Voice of **Brad Steiger**,
world renowned author

Gnosis, the Secret of Solomon's Temple Revealed
DVD
Find the true secret of the Knights Templar and the mysteries of the ancients. This is the story that has been kept from the ears of mankind for too long. You cannot truly live until you have Gnosis.

* The truth at the heart of ancient Freemasonry
* Who were Solomon and Sheba?
* The ancient and sacred nature of our quantum existence

57 minutes 24.95 USD

Secrets of the Serpent: In Search of the Sacred Past
DVD
Eons ago, an ancient serpent cult dominated mankind. Then, a great battle ensued and Christianity stamped it's authority on the face of the planet. Now, the real religious history of the world can be told. Philip Gardiner for the first time reveals:

* The world's most mysterious places were once sacred to the serpent cult.
* The secret of the Holy Grail and Elixir of Life
* The history and mythology of the so-called reptilian agenda

54 minutes 24.95 USD

RE Reality Press is a
division of
Reality Entertainment

www.reality-entertainment.com/books.htm

Printed in the United States
136089LV00003B/2/P

9 781934 588420